GREG NORMAN'S
GOLF CLASS

140 ILLUSTRATED
GOLF LESSONS

from the
SUNDAY EXPRESS

ISBN 0-85079 228-2

£2.99

CONTENTS

Introduction	3
Foreword by Greg Norman	4
BASICS	7
THE STANCE	11
THE GRIP	17
THE SWING	23
PUTTING	39
CHIPPING	49
WEDGE SHOTS	53
BUNKER SHOTS	55
THE ROUGH	63
TACTICS	69
WIND SHOTS	75
POSITIONING	81
PROBLEMS	89

Published by EXPRESS BOOKS, 245 Blackfriars Road, London SE1 9UX. Printed by Grosvenor Press (Portsmouth) Limited; Design: Philip Mann/ACE Ltd; Typeset by Dorchester Typesetting. Strips by John Andrisani. Drawings by Ken Lewis. © 1991 Great White Shark Enterprises.

INTRODUCTION

Sunday Express readers have, for several years now, been provided with a unique insight into golf the Greg Norman Way.

There are, he says, several good ways to swing at a golf ball, but only one good way to play golf – aggressively.

Aggressive play is a vital asset to the world's greatest golfers. It is even more important to the average player. Norman urges weekend golfers to attack the game in a bold, confident and determined manner. Then, he says, you will make a giant leap over the heads of your fellow players because most weekend golfers are anything but aggressive.

Norman, the 1986 Open Champion, and for many years ranked number one in the Sony World Rankings, shares the secrets of his own aggressive game through instructional strips showing golfers how to seize control of their own game and stop themselves being beaten either by their opponents or by the course.

Now a selection of Golf the Greg Norman Way has been packaged into this brilliant instructional book offering guidance on all aspects of the game . . .an invaluable guide for every golfer whatever your handicap mark.

Peter Watson, Sports Editor *Sunday Express*

FOREWORD

On any practice ground where the professionals warm up before tournament play you can be certain that tips will be freely exchanged; advice given.

These are the quiet moments that give tournament golf such fine fellowship and help to create a spirit that is unique to our ancient game.

Perhaps this is why I had great pleasure in putting this instructional book together. Everything I have said in my weekly strips in the Sunday Express comes from personal experience gathered since I first picked up a golf club to the present day. I hope you enjoy them and are able to have as much fun as I have had over the last few years.

You might be wondering why golf, more than any other sport, has inspired such a vast library covering a myriad of angles on instructional matters.

In many respects it is a game of romance and tradition and is played on courses set in beautiful surroundings. It can also be a difficult and tantalising pastime occasionally high on frustration.

Technique and understanding the swing are important elements of golf. Without being too technical I hope I have been able to convey some of the tricks of the trade I love so much.

My own first ever book was one written by my good friend Jack Nicklaus. I had never met him when I picked it up in my native Queensland where I used to caddy for my mother. It was a fascinating insight into the man the world knows as the Golden Bear and the way he plays the game.

4

In many ways it was my inspiration. After all no one in the world can match his record in the Majors and it is unlikely that anyone will accomplish anything approaching Jack's incredible number of feats.

As I read the book my thirst for knowledge increased even beyond what Jack was telling me and to this day I am still learning. In fact on long flights I usually have a copy of the Rules of Golf as one of my travelling companions so that I can store up the complexities of a particular aspect of the game.

These days Jack and I are neighbours in Florida. We often play together and in doing so we help each other spotting the occasional minor flaw that can creep unnoticed into anybody's swing.

One player I like to think I have helped is Sandy Lyle, that most amiable of men to play with. He was already an Open and US Masters champion when I met him on the practice ground at the Players' Championship at Ponte Vedra, Florida.

He was having problems. I asked him to hit a few balls and straight away I could see where the problem lay. I know he would have done the same for me.

The purpose of this book is to help you play better golf and there is not a golfer in the world who does not believe he has room for improvement.

Nick Faldo has risen to the very top because of his four Major victories but no-one works works harder to find that elusive perfection. He was already an outstanding tournament winner when he elected to change his swing under David Leadbetter.

It would be hard to find anyone as dedicated to improving himself. During his swing changes he would spend hours on the practice ground, working until his hands bled.

I have been through this routine myself, constantly chasing the perfect shot. I am not suggesting that the week-ender works until it hurts, but if the practice ground efforts are properly conducted, hitting on the range can be a lot of fun and ultimately productive.

I hope my tips are helpful. With just a little extra practice you should be able to take a stroke off your handicap.

I am a great advocate of arriving at the course early. Rushing to the tee, shoe-laces trailing is no way to prepare for a medal round. Make sure there is time to warm up, hit some balls and try to spend time on the putting green.

This, basically is the way the tournament professionals prepare for a round.

After a while this will become a habit as natural as brewing a cup of tea and cannot fail to bring about an improvement in anyone's game, especially the long-handicapper.

I hope the following pages will be an aid in handling the variety of surprises that crop up in every round from a difficult lie to a plugged bunker shot.

Keep your head down, think tempo and do your best to master par. Good luck.

Greg Norman

BASICS

BASICS

Basics

ONE OF THE MOST STRIKING IRONIES OF THE GAME OF GOLF, IS THAT THE AVERAGE AMATEUR WANTS TO PLAY LIKE A PRO, BUT HE DOESN'T WANT TO PRACTISE LIKE A PRO. DON'T MAKE THE SAME MISTAKE.

MAKE YOUR PRACTICE TIME COUNT BY DOING WHAT ALL FINE PLAYERS DO.

1. GO THROUGH A CONSISTENT PRE-SHOT ROUTINE;

2. CONCENTRATE INTENTLY, PRETENDING YOU ARE ON THE COURSE;

3. HIT SHOTS WITH A VARIETY OF CLUBS.

Golfer's lingo

IN CASE YOU'RE A GOLFER WHO IS CONFUSED BY INSTRUCTIONAL LINGO LET ME DEFINE A FEW VITAL TECHNICAL TERMS....

1. THE IMAGINARY LINE FROM THE BALL TO THE TARGET IS CALLED **THE TARGET LINE.**

TARGET LINE

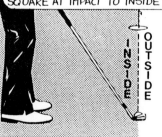

2. AS YOU SET UP, THE TERRITORY TO THE LEFT OF THE TARGET LINE IS CALLED **INSIDE.** THE TERRITORY TO THE RIGHT OF THE TARGET LINE IS CALLED **OUTSIDE.**
UNLESS YOU ARE PURPOSELY HITTING A LEFT TO RIGHT SHOT, YOU SHOULD SWING THE CLUB FROM INSIDE ON THE BACKSWING, TO SQUARE AT IMPACT TO INSIDE IN THE FOLLOW THROUGH.

INSIDE OUTSIDE

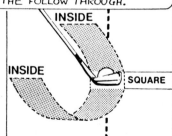

INSIDE

INSIDE

SQUARE

THE CORRECT SET-UP IS ESSENTIAL TO ANY GOOD GOLF SHOT, FOR IT PREDETERMINES THE SWING MOTION. TO HELP YOURSELF ADDRESS THE BALL BETTER, VISUALIZE A GOOD POSITION, AS YOU LINE UP THE SHOT, INITIALLY, FROM BEHIND THE BALL.

SEE YOURSELF STANDING COMFORTABLY ERECT....

WITH A SLIGHT BEND AT THE KNEES AND WAIST......

MAKE SURE, ALSO THAT YOU FEEL YOUR CHIN IS AWAY FROM YOUR CHEST, TOO. AND, MOST IMPORTANT, SEE THAT YOU'VE GIVEN YOURSELF PLENTY OF ROOM TO SWING THE CLUB FREELY BACK ON AN INSIDE PATH.

9

THE STANCE

The Stance

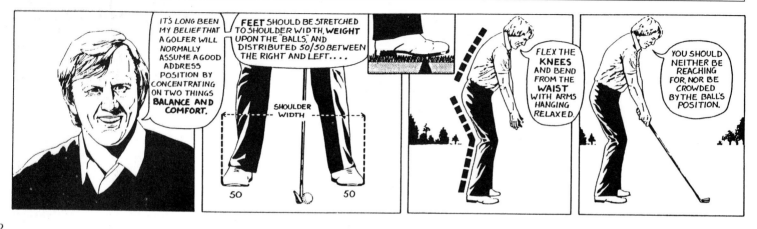

IT'S LONG BEEN MY BELIEF THAT A GOLFER WILL NORMALLY ASSUME A GOOD ADDRESS POSITION BY CONCENTRATING ON TWO THINGS **BALANCE AND COMFORT.**

FEET SHOULD BE STRETCHED TO SHOULDER WIDTH, **WEIGHT** UPON THE "BALLS," AND DISTRIBUTED 50/50 BETWEEN THE RIGHT AND LEFT....

SHOULDER WIDTH

50   50

FLEX THE **KNEES** AND BEND FROM THE **WAIST** WITH ARMS HANGING RELAXED.

YOU SHOULD NEITHER BE REACHING FOR, NOR BE CROWDED BY THE BALL'S POSITION.

12

Proper stance

MANY CLUB GOLFERS SWING BADLY AND HIT POOR MEDIUM IRON SHOTS INTO THE GREEN OWING TO AN OVERLY NARROW STANCE.

BECAUSE A NARROW STANCE CAUSES A PLAYER TO PICK THE CLUB VIRTUALLY STRAIGHT UP IN THE AIR, ON TOO STEEP A PLANE THE LIKELIHOOD IS THAT HE WILL CHOP DOWN, HITTING TOO ABRUPTLY INTO THE TURF BEHIND THE BALL.

HERE'S A GOOD GUIDE IN SETTING UP TO PLAY A MEDIUM IRON. SPREAD YOUR FEET SHOULDER-WIDTH APART TO PLAY THE FIVE IRON.

5 IRON

THEN, IN SELECTING A MORE LOFTED CLUB, NARROW THE STANCE SLIGHTLY. NOW, YOU'LL SWING THE CLUB CORRECTLY AND NIP THE BALL NICELY OFF THE TURF.

SHOULDER WIDTH

Perfect posture

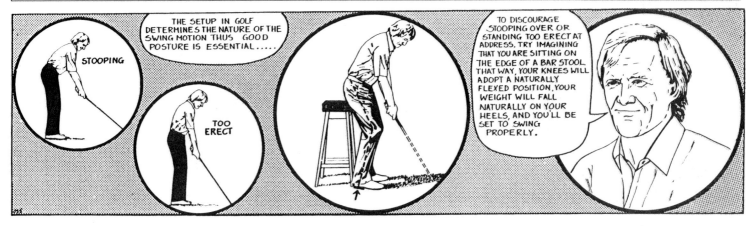

Alignment

THE STANCE

Toe the Line

THE ALIGNMENT OF YOUR SHOULDERS DICTATES THE PATH ON WHICH THE CLUB WILL SWING ALONG, ON THE BACKSWING AND DOWNSWING. TO MAKE CERTAIN THAT YOUR UPPER BODY IS LINED UP PROPERLY WITH REGARD TO YOUR TARGET, PLACE A CLUB ACROSS YOUR TOES PARALLEL TO THE TARGET-LINE. THEN, MAKE SURE THAT YOU SET EACH SHOULDER OVER THE CLUB......

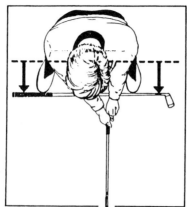

NOW YOU'LL SWING THE CLUB ON THE PROPER INSIDE—SQUARE—INSIDE PATH AND KNOCK YOUR SHOTS DEAD ON LINE.

Steady head

I HAD JUST AS MUCH TROUBLE KEEPING MY HEAD STILL WHEN TAKING UP GOLF AS THE NEXT GUY. FAILURE TO DO SO CAUSES A MULTITUDE OF PROBLEMS. FOR MANY PLAYERS

THE HEAD AND SPINE ARE THE AXIS THE SWING REVOLVES AROUND, SO ITS LOGICAL THAT KEEPING THEM IN ONE PLACE WILL MAXIMIZE YOUR CHANCES OF RETURNING THE CLUBHEAD SQUARELY TO THE BALL ON THE DOWNSWING.

Hitting a Draw

CLOSE YOUR STANCE BY DRAWING YOUR **RIGHT** FOOT ABOUT TWO INCHES BACK; LIKEWISE THE HIPS AND SHOULDERS, SO THE THE BODY IS AIMED RIGHT OF THE TARGET.

DRAW

ALTHOUGH I PREFER TO PLAY THE BALL FROM LEFT TO RIGHT I WOULDN'T HAVE ACHIEVED THE TOURNAMENT SUCCESS I HAVE IF I COULDN'T **DRAW** THE BALL, TOO........

TARGET LINE

AIM THE CLUBFACE DIRECTLY AT THE TARGET AND SWING NORMALLY.

15

Hitting a Fade

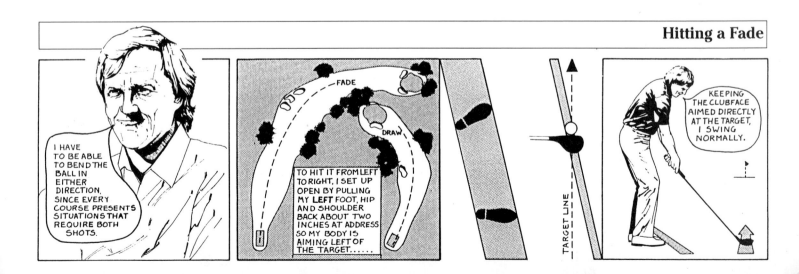

I HAVE TO BE ABLE TO BEND THE BALL IN EITHER DIRECTION, SINCE EVERY COURSE PRESENTS SITUATIONS THAT REQUIRE BOTH SHOTS.

FADE

DRAW

TO HIT IT FROM LEFT TO RIGHT, I SET UP OPEN BY PULLING MY **LEFT** FOOT, HIP AND SHOULDER BACK ABOUT TWO INCHES AT ADDRESS SO MY BODY IS AIMING LEFT OF THE TARGET......

TARGET LINE

KEEPING THE CLUBFACE AIMED DIRECTLY AT THE TARGET, I SWING NORMALLY.

Plane of action

16

THE GRIP

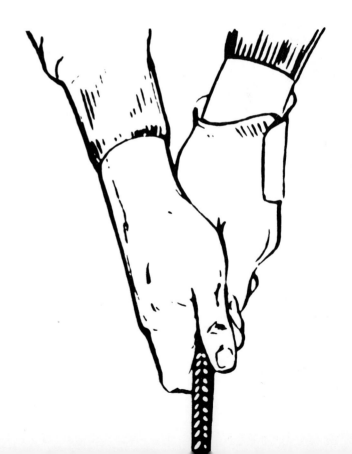

THE GRIP

The Grip

I CONSIDER THE GRIP TO BE THE ENGINE ROOM OF THE SWING, LARGELY BECAUSE HOLDING THE CLUB PROPERLY IS ESSENTIAL TO GENERATING CLUBHEAD SPEED AND ACHIEVING SQUARE CLUBFACE TO BALL CONTACT, AT IMPACT..........

SO, WEDGE THE CLUB'S BUTT END AGAINST THE PAD OF THE LEFT HAND WITH THE LAST TWO FINGERS.

WHILE GRIPPING MAINLY WITH THE FINGERS OF THE RIGHT.......

AT ADDRESS ABOUT 2½ KNUCKLES SHOULD BE VISIBLE ON THE LEFT HAND, AND 2 KNUCKLES ON THE RIGHT AS YOU LOOK DOWN.

2 KNUCKLES

2½ KNUCKLES

NOW YOU ARE IN THE BEST POSITION TO MAKE BEST SWING

18

Gripping the club

PUTTING YOUR HANDS ON THE CLUB PROPERLY IS VERY CRITICAL TO HITTING A DRIVE TO A DESIGNATED TARGET YOU'VE PICKED A COUPLE OF HUNDRED YARDS OR MORE OUT IN THE FAIRWAY.

WHETHER YOU ADOPT AN INTERLOCK, OVERLAP OR BASEBALL HOLD, WHEN YOU LOOK DOWN AT ADDRESS YOU SHOULD BE ABLE TO SEE TWO - TWO AND A HALF KNUCKLES OF YOUR LEFT HAND. ALSO, BOTH PALMS SHOULD BE PARALLEL TO EACH OTHER.

FUTHERMORE YOUR LEFT WRIST SHOULD BE RELATIVELY STRAIGHT IF IT'S CONVEXED THE TENDENCY IS TO LIFT THE CLUB STRAIGHT UP AT THE START OF THE SWING ON AN OVERLY STEEP PLANE, WHICH CAUSES A SLICE. SO GET A HOLD ON YOUR GRIP.

SHOWING MORE OF THE KNUCKLES OF YOUR LEFT HAND AND TURNING YOUR RIGHT HAND TOO FAR UNDER THE CLUB, WILL LEAD TO AN OVERLY FLAT SWING THAT CAUSES A VIOLENT HOOK SHOT.

2½

Grip pressure

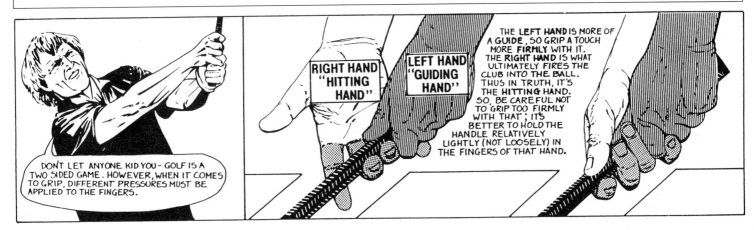

DON'T LET ANYONE KID YOU – GOLF IS A TWO SIDED GAME. HOWEVER, WHEN IT COMES TO GRIP, DIFFERENT PRESSURES MUST BE APPLIED TO THE FINGERS.

RIGHT HAND "HITTING HAND"

LEFT HAND "GUIDING HAND"

THE **LEFT HAND** IS MORE OF A GUIDE, SO GRIP A TOUCH MORE **FIRMLY** WITH IT. THE **RIGHT HAND** IS WHAT ULTIMATELY FIRES THE CLUB INTO THE BALL. THUS IN TRUTH, IT'S THE **HITTING HAND**. SO, BE CAREFUL NOT TO 'GRIP TOO FIRMLY WITH THAT'; IT'S BETTER TO HOLD THE HANDLE RELATIVELY LIGHTLY (NOT LOOSELY) IN THE FINGERS OF THAT HAND.

19

Hand position

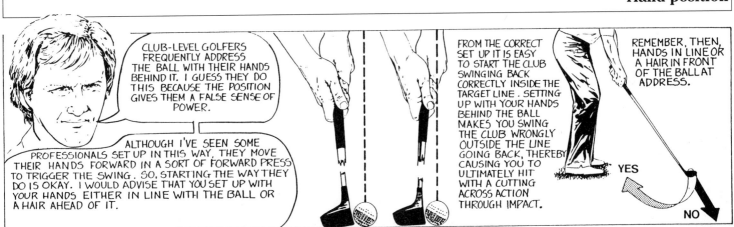

CLUB-LEVEL GOLFERS FREQUENTLY ADDRESS THE BALL WITH THEIR HANDS BEHIND IT. I GUESS THEY DO THIS BECAUSE THE POSITION GIVES THEM A FALSE SENSE OF POWER.

ALTHOUGH I'VE SEEN SOME PROFESSIONALS SET UP IN THIS WAY, THEY MOVE THEIR HANDS FORWARD IN A SORT OF FORWARD PRESS TO TRIGGER THE SWING. SO, STARTING THE WAY THEY DO IS OKAY. I WOULD ADVISE THAT YOU SET UP WITH YOUR HANDS EITHER IN LINE WITH THE BALL OR A HAIR AHEAD OF IT.

FROM THE CORRECT SET UP IT IS EASY TO START THE CLUB SWINGING BACK CORRECTLY INSIDE THE TARGET LINE. SETTING UP WITH YOUR HANDS BEHIND THE BALL MAKES YOU SWING THE CLUB WRONGLY OUTSIDE THE LINE GOING BACK, THEREBY CAUSING YOU TO ULTIMATELY HIT WITH A CUTTING ACROSS ACTION THROUGH IMPACT.

REMEMBER, THEN, HANDS IN LINE OR A HAIR IN FRONT OF THE BALL AT ADDRESS.

YES

NO

Watch your hands

MOST AMATEUR GOLFERS REALISE THAT THE WOODS, LONG IRONS AND MEDIUM IRONS CALL FOR A FLAT PLANE OF BACK-SWING AND A SWEEPING ACTION THROUGH IMPACT; WHERE AS THE SHORT IRONS CALL FOR AN UPRIGHT BACKSWING AND DESCENDING BLOW AT IMPACT. YET FEW PLAYERS KNOW THAT IT'S THE POSITION OF THE HAND AT ADDRESS THAT DICTATE THE CORRECT PLANE AND HIT.

TO PROMOTE A SHALLOW SWING AND SWEEP TRY THE FOLLOWING.....

.... PLAY THE BALL OFF YOUR LEFT HEEL AND HAVE YOUR HANDS LINED UP WITH THE BALL. WHEN PLAYING THE SHORT IRONS MOVE THE BALL BACK TOWARDS THE MIDDLE OF YOUR STANCE SO YOUR HANDS ARE SET A COUPLE OF INCHES AHEAD OF THE BALL.

Quieten your hands

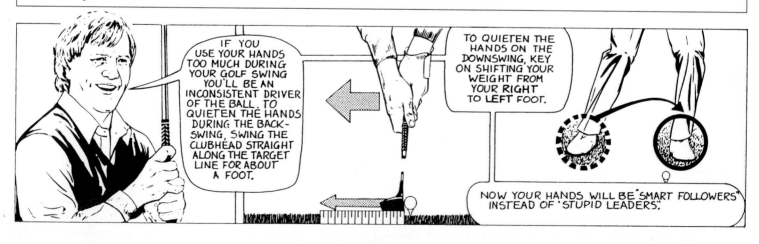

IF YOU USE YOUR HANDS TOO MUCH DURING YOUR GOLF SWING YOU'LL BE AN INCONSISTENT DRIVER OF THE BALL. TO QUIETEN THE HANDS DURING THE BACK-SWING, SWING THE CLUBHEAD STRAIGHT ALONG THE TARGET LINE FOR ABOUT A FOOT.

TO QUIETEN THE HANDS ON THE DOWNSWING, KEY ON SHIFTING YOUR WEIGHT FROM YOUR RIGHT TO LEFT FOOT.

NOW YOUR HANDS WILL BE "SMART FOLLOWERS" INSTEAD OF "STUPID LEADERS".

Release the hands

TO GET MAXIMUM DISTANCE AND ACCURACY FROM YOUR SWING YOUR **HANDS** HAVE TO **RELEASE** PROPERLY THROUGH THE **HITTING ZONE.** FAILURE TO **RELEASE** RESULTS IN "BLOCKING," USUALLY CAUSING AN OPEN FACE AT IMPACT, MAKING THE BALL GO RIGHT...

BLOCKING

..TO RELEASE PROPERLY, IMAGINE MAKING THE TOE OF THE CLUB PASS THE HEEL AS IT MOVES THROUGH THE BALL...

THIS WILL PPODUCE THE CORRECT **COUNTER-CLOCKWISE** FOREARM ROTATION AND HAND ACTION YOU WANT.

Wrist action

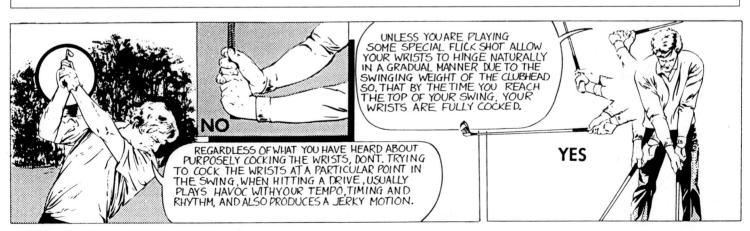

NO

UNLESS YOU ARE PLAYING SOME SPECIAL FLICK SHOT ALLOW YOUR WRISTS TO HINGE NATURALLY IN A GRADUAL MANNER DUE TO THE SWINGING WEIGHT OF THE CLUBHEAD SO. THAT BY THE TIME YOU REACH THE TOP OF YOUR SWING, YOUR WRISTS ARE FULLY COCKED.

YES

REGARDLESS OF WHAT YOU HAVE HEARD ABOUT PURPOSELY COCKING THE WRISTS, DON'T. TRYING TO COCK THE WRISTS AT A PARTICULAR POINT IN THE SWING, WHEN HITTING A DRIVE, USUALLY PLAYS HAVOC WITH YOUR TEMPO, TIMING AND RHYTHM, AND ALSO PRODUCES A JERKY MOTION.

THE SWING

The Backswing

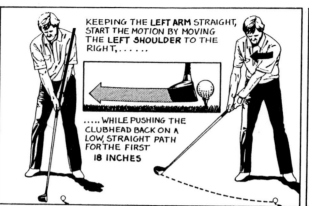

I'VE SEEN FEW PLAYERS MAKE A GOOD DOWNSWING AFTER A POOR BACKSWING

KEEPING THE **LEFT ARM** STRAIGHT, START THE MOTION BY MOVING THE **LEFT SHOULDER** TO THE RIGHT, ...

. . . . . WHILE PUSHING THE CLUBHEAD BACK ON A LOW, STRAIGHT PATH FOR THE FIRST 18 INCHES

90°

LET THE WRISTS COCK TO NO MORE THAN A 90 DEGREE ANGLE AT THE TOP.

24

One backswing key

TO MAKE A GOOD BACKSWING, THINK OF SWINGING YOUR **HANDS UP OVER YOUR RIGHT SHOULDER**.

TWO THINGS ARE ACHIEVED BY DOING THIS: (1) YOU'LL SWING THE CLUB ON A GOOD PLANE...

(2) YOU'LL MAKE A STRONG, POWERFUL TURN AWAY FROM THE BALL...

YOU'LL PUT YOURSELF IN A STRONG POSITION AT THE TOP TO UNCOIL INTO THE DOWNSWING POWERFULLY AND BRING THE CLUB THROUGH ON A GOOD SWING PATH.

Compact backswing

WHEN I FIRST STARTED PLAYING TOUR GOLF I LOST VITAL STROKES AND VALUABLE PRIZE MONEY BECAUSE I HIT THE BALL WILD OFF THE TEE. THE CAUSE: I SWUNG THE CLUB BACK WELL BEYOND THE CLASSIC PARALLEL POSITION. DON'T YOU.

GAIN CONTROL BY MAKING A COMPACT BACKSWING. SWING TO THE THREE-QUARTER POINT OR TO THE PARALLEL POINT, IF LIKE ME YOU POSSESS GOOD FLEXIBILITY.

BEING IN THE CONTROL POSITION AT THE TOP OF THE SWING MAY COST YOU SOME DISTANCE OFF THE TEE. BUT WHAT IS A COUPLE OF YARDS DIFFERENCE IF YOUR'E HITTING FROM THE FAIRWAY INSTEAD OF THE ROUGH?

Slow start, be smart

A QUICK TAKEAWAY IS ALWAYS DANGEROUS, SIMPLY BECAUSE IT PREVENTS THE BODY FROM WORKING IN HARMONY. THE PLAYER WHO SNAPS THE CLUB BACK AT THE START OF THE SWING TENDS TO SWAY OFF THE BALL. A SLOW TEMPO, BY CONTRAST, SETS UP AN EFFECTIVE TEMPO FOR THE ENTIRE SWING AND A COORDINATED BODY ACTION........

SNAP = SWAY

I CONCENTRATE ON GOING BACK VERY SLOW AND SO SHOULD YOU, FOR THIS SMOOTH TAKEAWAY WILL ALLOW YOU TO TURN FULLY....

FEEL THE POSITION OF YOUR HANDS AT THE TOP AND MAKE A SMOOTH TRANSITION INTO THE DOWNSWING.

SLOW

THE SWING

Strong turn for power

EVERY TOUR PLAYER BELIEVES THAT A STRONG UPPER BODY COIL IS THE KEY TO GENERATING POWER. HOWEVER, I HAVE FOUND FROM TALKING TO AMATEURS THAT, THEY HAVE TROUBLE "TURNING THEIR BACKS TO THE HOLE" AS TEACHERS COMMONLY SUGGEST....

...A BETTER SUGGESTION FOR ENCOURAGING A MORE POWERFUL TURN IS TO THINK OF TURNING THE CENTRE OF YOUR CHEST AWAY, SO AT THE TOP OF THE MOTION THE CENTRE OF THE CHEST FACES AWAY FROM THE TARGET..

TARGET

...THIS TIP WILL ALSO ENCOURAGE YOU TO CLEAR YOUR RIGHT HIP OUT OF THE WAY. ON THE BACKSWING, THUS SETTING UP A CLEAR PATH FOR THE ARMS AND CLUB TO SWING ALONG.

At the Top

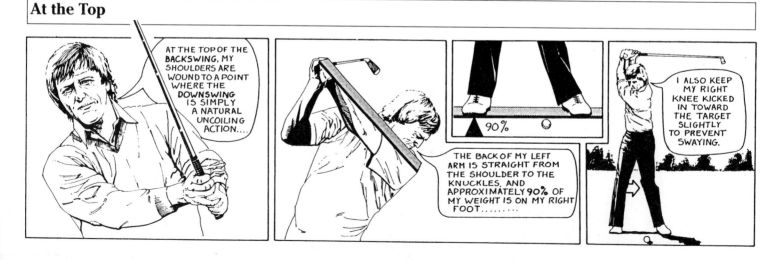

AT THE TOP OF THE BACKSWING, MY SHOULDERS ARE WOUND TO A POINT WHERE THE DOWNSWING IS SIMPLY A NATURAL UNCOILING ACTION....

90%

THE BACK OF MY LEFT ARM IS STRAIGHT FROM THE SHOULDER TO THE KNUCKLES, AND APPROXIMATELY 90% OF MY WEIGHT IS ON MY RIGHT FOOT........

I ALSO KEEP MY RIGHT KNEE KICKED IN TOWARD THE TARGET SLIGHTLY TO PREVENT SWAYING.

From the Top

THE POSITION THE CLUB ARRIVES IN AT THE TOP OF THE SWING HAS A LOT TO DO WITH THE TYPE OF SHOT YOU HIT. IDEALLY, AT THE TOP, THE CLUBSHAFT SHOULD BE PARALLEL TO THE TARGET LINE. THEREFORE, EITHER LOOK AT A MIRROR TO CHECK YOUR POSITION, OR HAVE A FRIEND STAND BEHIND YOU AND ANALYZE YOUR AT THE TOP POSITION.

IF THE SHAFT POINTS TO THE **LEFT** OF YOUR TARGET YOU WILL SWING INTO IMPACT FROM THE **OUTSIDE** AND THUS START THE BALL FLYING **LEFT** OF YOUR TARGET. IF THE SHAFT POINTS **RIGHT** OF YOUR TARGET AT THE TOP, YOU WILL SWING INTO IMPACT FROM TOO FAR **INSIDE** AND START THE BALL FLYING TO THE **RIGHT** OF TARGET.

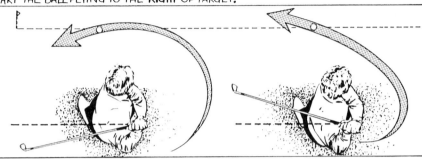

27

The Downswing

LIKE MOST PROS, MY **LEGS** AND **HIPS** PLAY A BIG PART IN THE **DOWNSWING** TO HELP GENERATE CLUBHEAD SPEED......

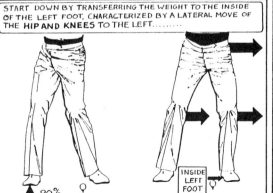

START DOWN BY TRANSFERRING THE WEIGHT TO THE INSIDE OF THE LEFT FOOT, CHARACTERIZED BY A LATERAL MOVE OF THE **HIP** AND **KNEES** TO THE LEFT.........

90%

INSIDE LEFT FOOT

THE SHOULDERS UNWIND IMMEDIATELY AFTER,

ALLOWING THE ARMS TO SWING THE CLUB QUICKLY THROUGH THE BALL.

THE SWING

Break the ball blind

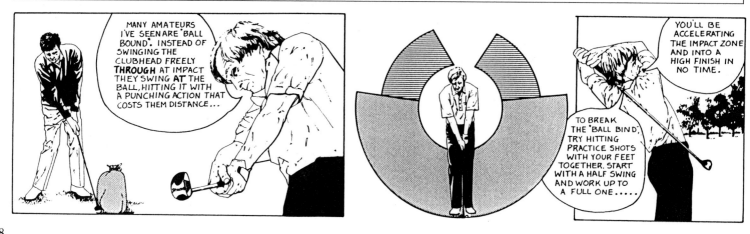

Slow but sure

First move down

AMATEUR GOLFERS OFTEN ASK ME WHAT THE FIRST MOVE ON THE DOWNSWING SHOULD BE. WELL, THAT DEPENDS ON THE POSITION THE CLUBFACE IS IN AT THE TOP OF THE SWING.

SQUARE OPEN

IF YOU HAVE THE CLUBFACE SQUARE OR OPEN YOU SHOULD KEY ON PULLING THE BUTT OF THE LEFT HAND VIRTUALLY STRAIGHT DOWN.

HOWEVER IF YOU ARRIVE AT THE TOP WITH THE CLUBFACE IN A CLOSED POSITION YOU SHOULD KEY ON MOVING YOUR LEFT SIDE TO THE LEFT.......

CLOSED

.....OPENING A PATH FOR THE ARMS TO SWING THROUGH FREELY.

29

Swing through the ball

IF A HIGH PERCENT OF YOUR TEE SHOTS FLY INTO TROUBLE TO THE RIGHT SIDE OF THE FAIRWAY YOU ARE PROBABLY FAILING TO SWING THROUGH THE BALL INSTEAD YOU ARE HITTING "AT" IT, WHICH IS ONE FAULT SHARED BY MANY AMATEURS.

TO ACCELERATE THE CLUB IN THE HITTING AREA, SO THAT AT IMPACT IT'S MOVING AT FULL SPEED.

THINK OF SWINGING INTO A FULL FINISH BEFORE YOU EVEN PULL THE TRIGGER.

NO

YES

THE SWING

The Follow-through

MANY HANDICAP GOLFERS I'VE SEEN DON'T FOLLOW THROUGH CORRECTLY, INSTEAD DECELERATING INTO THE BALL.

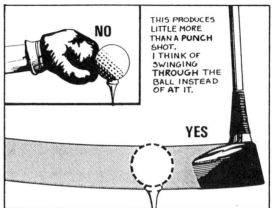

NO

THIS PRODUCES LITTLE MORE THAN A PUNCH SHOT. I THINK OF SWINGING THROUGH THE BALL INSTEAD OF AT IT.

YES

I FINISH WITH MY HANDS HIGH, CHEST FACING THE TARGET, AND WEIGHT ON THE OUTSIDE MY LEFT FOOT. IF I DIDN'T DO THIS, I'D NEVER GET THE DISTANCE I NEED.

Straight to the ball

TAKING THE CLUB BACK STRAIGHT-AWAY FROM THE BALL MAKES IT EASIER TO SWING STRAIGHT-THROUGH IT ON THE DOWNSWING. TO HELP MAKE A GOOD TAKE AWAY, PICK OUT A SPOT ABOUT A FOOT DIRECTLY BEHIND THE BALL......

...CONCENTRATE ON TAKING THE CLUB BACK BY PUSHING YOUR LEFT ELBOW AWAY FROM THE TARGET. THIS GIVES A STRAIGHT AND EXTENDED TAKE-AWAY, ELIMINATING EXCESSIVE HAND MOTION AWAY FROM THE BALL.

CORRECT

12 inches

INCORRECT

Stop the sway

A LOT OF GOLFERS WHO HIT WAYWARD TEE SHOTS AND APPROACHES WIDE OF THE GREEN DO SO BECAUSE THEY MOVE THE LOWER BODY LATERALLY ON THE BACKSWING INSTEAD OF TURNING IT AROUND THE FIXED AXIS OF SPINE. WHEN YOU DO THIS IT'S HARD TO TIME THE DOWNSWING AND PUT THE CLUB SQUARELY ON THE BALL . . . .

A BAD SWAY

A GOOD TURN

FIXED AXIS

TO GROOVE THE RIGHT BACKSWING MOVEMENT, FOR POWERFUL AND ACCURATE SHOTS, TRY HITTING BALLS WITH A GOLF BALL PLACED UNDER THE HEEL OF YOUR RIGHT FOOT. THIS ENCOURAGES YOU TO SHIFT YOUR WEIGHT TO THE INSIDE OF YOUR RIGHT FOOT AND TO KEEP YOUR RIGHT LEG "BRACED". FROM THIS POSITION YOU CAN'T POSSIBLY SWAY.

31

Stop swaying

SWAYING TO THE RIGHT ON THE BACKSWING IS A COMMON FAULT THAT ALMOST ALWAYS LEADS TO INCONSISTENT BALL-STRIKING...

TO GUARD AGAINST IT, KICK YOUR RIGHT KNEE INWARD AT ADDRESS AND KEEP IT THAT WAY THROUGHOUT THE BACKSWING

IT WILL ACT AS A BRACE AGAINST LETTING YOUR BODY MOVE AWAY FROM THE BALL.

THE SWING

Rock and roll

THE BEST AVENUE TO A POWERFUL GOLF SWING IS BUILDING A SOLID FOUNDATION IN YOUR FEET AND ANKLES — ONE THAT WILL CONTROL THE BALANCE AND TEMPO OF YOUR SWING.

HERE'S HOW TO DANCE YOUR WAY TO DISTANCE: ON THE BACKSWING, ROLL YOUR LEFT ANKLE IN TOWARDS YOUR RIGHT FOOT.

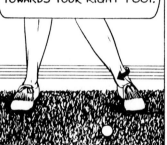

TRIGGER THE DOWNSWING BY ROLLING YOUR LEFT ANKLE TOWARDS THE TARGET. NOW YOUR RIGHT ANKLE WILL ROLL IN TOWARD THE TARGET, MAKING FOR A STRONG RIGHT SIDED HIT ON IMPACT.

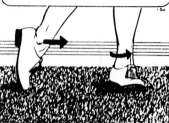

Easy does it

THE MOST COMMON FAULT HIGH HANDICAPPERS MAKE IS SWINGING TOO FAST, AND THAT'S WHY THEIR TEE SHOTS FLY SO WILDLY OFF-LINE. EITHER FAR LEFT OR FAR RIGHT.

IF YOU THINK YOU SUFFER WITH THIS FAULT WHISPER

LOW AND SLOW

TO HELP YOU DRAG THE CLUB QUITE LOW TO THE GROUND IN THE TAKEAWAY.

DO THAT AND YOU WILL GRADUALLY BUILD UP CLUB HEAD SPEED MAKING FOR STRAIGHTER AND MORE SOLID HITS.

Helpful Swing Hook

ONE SURE WAY TO FREEZE OVER A SHOT AND MAKE A POOR SWING IS TO THINK TOO MUCH ABOUT TECHNIQUE. EVEN I NEED A SWING KEY, BUT I KEEP THEM TO A MINIMUM.

HERE'S ONE PRESWING TECHNICAL "HOOK" THAT WILL HELP YOU SWING WITH BETTER RHYTHM AND TEMPO.

ENVISAGE YOURSELF MAKING A PERFECT BACKSWING AND DOWNSWING. THIS ONE VISUAL IMAGE WILL ENCOURAGE YOU TO SWING THE CLUB BACK TO THE PARALLEL POSITION AT THE TOP AND THEN NICELY DOWN AND THROUGH THE BALL.

Wide swing

ONE OF THE BEST AVENUES TO CREATING POWER IS TO BUILD A WIDE ARC OF SWING, IN ORDER TO ACCOMPLISH THIS GOAL.....
1. SET UP SO THAT YOUR LEFT ARM AND CLUB-SHAFT FORM A STRAIGHT LINE.

2. MAKE A ONE-PIECE TAKEAWAY, MOVING YOUR ARMS AND CLUBHEAD BACK, AWAY FROM THE TARGET SIMULTANEOUSLY;

3. CONTINUE DRAGGING THE CLUB BACK LOW TO THE GROUND WELL BEYOND YOUR RIGHT FOOT, OR UNTIL YOU FEEL MOST OF YOUR WEIGHT SHIFTS TO THE INSIDE OF YOUR RIGHT FOOT.

NOW IF YOU CONTINUE UP, THE WIDTH OF YOUR SWING WILL BE FAR GREATER THAN IT WOULD BE IF YOU NARROWED THE ARC BY VIOLENTLY BREAKING YOUR WRISTS AND PICKING THE CLUB STRAIGHT UP.

THE SWING

No more Overswing

"OVERSWINGING" WITH WOODS AND LONG IRONS RESULTS IN LOSS OF CLUB HEAD CONTROL, USUALLY CAUSING A POOR DOWNSWING PATH AND A MISDIRECTED SHOT......

IT USUALLY STEMS FROM TRYING TO TAKE THE CLUB BACK A LITTLE FARTHER TO HIT THE BALL HARDER. TO STOP, IMAGINE YOU'RE SWINGING A 5-IRON INSTEAD OF A LONGER CLUB....

YOU'LL MAKE A MORE COMPACT, CONTROLLED SWING AND HIT THE SHOT STRAIGHTER.

Swing on an upright plane

HOOKING OFTEN RESULTS FROM SWINGING ON TOO FLAT A PLANE. TRAIN YOURSELF TO MAKE A MORE UPRIGHT SWING BY SETTING UP WITH A WALL ABOUT EIGHTEEN INCHES BEHIND YOU....

SQUARE YOUR HEELS TO THE WALL, AND PRACTICE YOUR SWING. IF YOUR SWING IS TOO FLAT YOU'LL HIT THE WALL WITH THE CLUB ON THE BACKSWING;

SO TO AVOID THAT YOU'LL BE FORCED TO DEVELOP A MORE UPRIGHT SWING PATH.

Get hip

Turn the hips

THE SWING

Left foot lift

Build your hitting power

The big body coil

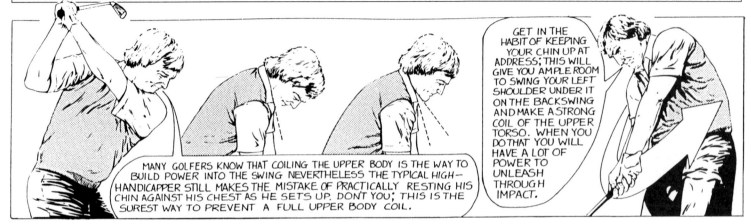

MANY GOLFERS KNOW THAT COILING THE UPPER BODY IS THE WAY TO BUILD POWER INTO THE SWING NEVERTHELESS THE TYPICAL HIGH-HANDICAPPER STILL MAKES THE MISTAKE OF PRACTICALLY RESTING HIS CHIN AGAINST HIS CHEST AS HE SETS UP. DON'T YOU; THIS IS THE SUREST WAY TO PREVENT A FULL UPPER BODY COIL.

GET IN THE HABIT OF KEEPING YOUR CHIN UP AT ADDRESS; THIS WILL GIVE YOU AMPLE ROOM TO SWING YOUR LEFT SHOULDER UNDER IT ON THE BACKSWING AND MAKE A STRONG COIL OF THE UPPER TORSO. WHEN YOU DO THAT YOU WILL HAVE A LOT OF POWER TO UNLEASH THROUGH IMPACT.

Power key

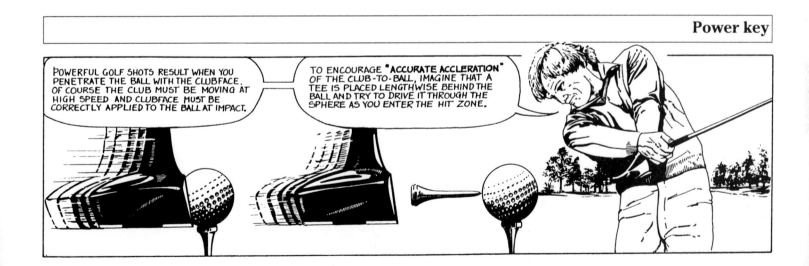

POWERFUL GOLF SHOTS RESULT WHEN YOU PENETRATE THE BALL WITH THE CLUBFACE. OF COURSE THE CLUB MUST BE MOVING AT HIGH SPEED AND CLUBFACE MUST BE CORRECTLY APPLIED TO THE BALL AT IMPACT.

TO ENCOURAGE "ACCURATE ACCLERATION" OF THE CLUB-TO-BALL, IMAGINE THAT A TEE IS PLACED LENGTHWISE BEHIND THE BALL AND TRY TO DRIVE IT THROUGH THE SPHERE AS YOU ENTER THE HIT ZONE.

THE SWING

Groove a late hit

Parallel position

38

PUTTING

PUTTING

Putting pointers

I'VE SEEN MANY DIFFERENT TYPES OF PUTTING STROKES GET THE JOB DONE.....

...FROM ARM AND SHOULDER METHODS TO WRISTY ONES.

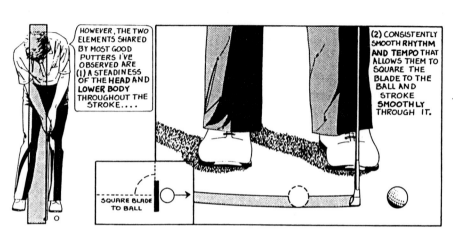

HOWEVER, THE TWO ELEMENTS SHARED BY MOST GOOD PUTTERS I'VE OBSERVED ARE (1) A STEADINESS OF THE HEAD AND LOWER BODY THROUGHOUT THE STROKE....

(2) CONSISTENTLY SMOOTH RHYTHM AND TEMPO THAT ALLOWS THEM TO SQUARE THE BLADE TO THE BALL AND STROKE SMOOTHLY THROUGH IT.

SQUARE BLADE TO BALL

One Putting must

JACK NICKLAUS

BERNHARD LANGER

PUTTING IS THE MOST INDIVIDUALISTIC DEPARTMENT OF THE GAME. IF YOU NEED PROOF OF THIS, JUST WATCH THE PROS OR EVEN YOUR AMATEUR PLAYING PARTNERS, AND YOU WILL SEE HOW THEIR STROKES VARY.

ALL THE SAME, GREAT PLAYERS SHARE ONE BASIC PUTTING KEY: THEIR HEADS STAY PERFECTLY STILL.

YOU TOO, SHOULD KEEP YOUR HEAD STEADY DURING THE BACKSTROKE AND DOWNSTROKE. YOU WILL THEN HIT MORE SOLID, ON-LINE PUTTS.

Check your Putting set-up

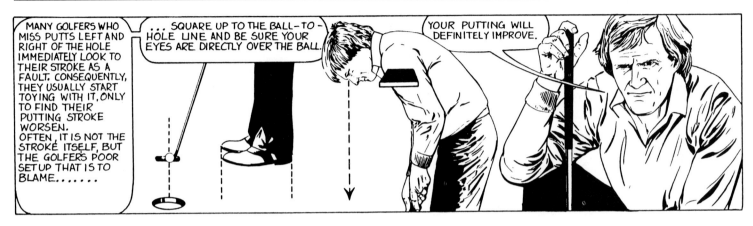

MANY GOLFERS WHO MISS PUTTS LEFT AND RIGHT OF THE HOLE IMMEDIATELY LOOK TO THEIR STROKE AS A FAULT. CONSEQUENTLY, THEY USUALLY START TOYING WITH IT, ONLY TO FIND THEIR PUTTING STROKE WORSEN.
OFTEN, IT IS NOT THE STROKE ITSELF, BUT THE GOLFER'S POOR SET UP THAT IS TO BLAME.......

... SQUARE UP TO THE BALL-TO-HOLE LINE AND BE SURE YOUR EYES ARE DIRECTLY OVER THE BALL.

YOUR PUTTING WILL DEFINITELY IMPROVE.

41

Short Putts

NEARLY EVERY GOLFER IS PLAGUED BY THE **YIPS** AT SOME POINT, BUT THIS DRILL CAN GET YOU BACK ON TRACK:

FIND A STRAIGHT THREE FOOTER AND PRACTISE IT, MAKING SURE TO COMPLETE EACH STROKE WITH A **LONG FOLLOW-THROUGH** STRAIGHT TO THE HOLE, CONTINUING IT UNTIL THE BALL DROPS INTO THE HOLE...

.... THIS FORCES YOU TO ACCELERATE EVENLY THROUGH THE BALL WHILE KEEPING THE FACE SQUARE AT IMPACT.

PUTTING

Long Putt strategy

I RARELY STEP UP TO A 40 FOOTER EXPECTING TO MAKE IT.... THAT'S PUTTING TOO MUCH PRESSURE ON MYSELF....

... IF YOU'RE GUILTY OF THIS AND HAVING TROUBLE GETTING THE LONG ONES CLOSE, TRY IMAGINING A CIRCLE AROUND THE HOLE SIX FEET IN DIAMETER. IF YOU GET WITHIN THAT TARGET, YOU'LL BE LEFT WITH A 3 FOOTER AT MOST.

3' — 3'

Up front Putting

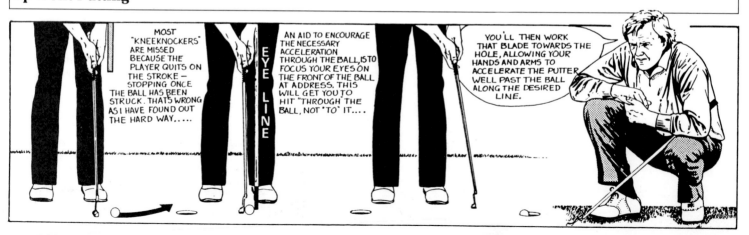

MOST "KNEEKNOCKERS" ARE MISSED BECAUSE THE PLAYER QUITS ON THE STROKE — STOPPING ONCE THE BALL HAS BEEN STRUCK. THAT'S WRONG AS I HAVE FOUND OUT THE HARD WAY.....

EYE LINE

AN AID TO ENCOURAGE THE NECESSARY ACCELERATION THROUGH THE BALL, IS TO FOCUS YOUR EYES ON THE FRONT OF THE BALL AT ADDRESS. THIS WILL GET YOU TO HIT "THROUGH" THE BALL, NOT "TO" IT....

YOU'LL THEN WORK THAT BLADE TOWARDS THE HOLE, ALLOWING YOUR HANDS AND ARMS TO ACCELERATE THE PUTTER WELL PAST THE BALL ALONG THE DESIRED LINE.

Spot Putting

MANY AMATEUR GOLFERS THAT I'VE BEEN PAIRED WITH IN PRO-AM TOURNAMENTS HAVE EXCELLENT PUTTING STROKES, YET MISS ON EITHER THE LEFT OR RIGHT SIDE OF THE HOLE.

THE REASON: THEIR AIMING IS OFF.

IF YOU HAVE DIFFICULTY LINING YOURSELF UP, PICK A SPOT IN THE GRASS A FEW INCHES IN FRONT OF THE BALL NEXT, SET SQUARE TO THAT SPOT AIMING TO PUTT OVER IT. BECAUSE YOUR INTERIM TARGET SPOT IS CLOSER TO YOU, YOUR AIM AND CONFIDENCE WILL IMPROVE.

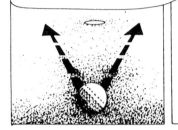

43

Long Putting keys

ALIGNING YOURSELF CORRECTLY AT ADDRESS, HITTING TO A SPECIFIC SPOT AND PACING THE BALL TO THE CUP ARE KEY ELEMENTS FOR GOOD LONG PUTTING, ESPECIALLY WHEN THE BALL BREAKS SEVERELY.

I FIND THAT AIMING AT THREE SEPERATE SPOTS TO THE LEFT OF THE HOLE AND THREE SPOTS TO THE RIGHT OF THE HOLE (EACH SPREAD ONE INCH APART) ON 25 TO 30 FOOT PUTTS, HELPS ME GROOVE A GREAT ALIGNMENT IN ADDITION ENHANCING MY VISUALIZATION OF THE BALL TO TARGET LINE.

Putting in wind

SOME PLAYERS DON'T REALIZE THAT A STRONG WIND CAN TRULY AFFECT THE ROLL OF YOUR BALL THE WIND MAY ONLY THROW THE BALL A HAIR OFF COARSE, BUT ON THE GREENS THAT CAN MEAN THE DIFFERENCE BETWEEN MISSING AND MAKING A PUTT. SO WHEN PUTTING INTO A STRONG HEADWIND:

1. STAND WITH YOUR FEET SPREAD FARTHER APART FOR BETTER BALANCE;

2. EXAGGERATE THE BEND IN YOUR KNEES FOR BETTER LEVERAGE;

3. MAKE A STRONGER, BUT FIRMER STROKE.

Putter-power

THE AVERAGE CLUB PLAYER OFTEN TRIES TOO HARD TO PICK HIS CHIPS PERFECTLY CLEANLY OFF THE FRINGE GRASS. THE TENDENCY, USING SUCH A TECHNIQUE, IS TO SKULL THE BALL. THE BEST THING YOU CAN DO IS TO REALIZE THAT THE PUTTER IS THE BEST CLUB TO PLAY FROM A GOOD LIE, JUST OFF THE FRINGE.

. . . . SO, JUST BECAUSE THE BALL ISN'T ON THE GREEN, DON'T AUTOMATICALLY REACH FOR AN IRON CLUB . . . . .

. . . . . A PUTTER WILL DISCOURAGE YOU FROM TRYING TO HELP THE BALL UP IN THE AIR. MORE OVER, YOU'LL PREVENT YOURSELF SKULLING THE BALL OVER THE GREEN; INSTEAD YOU'LL LEAVE YOURSELF AN EASY PAR-SAVING "SECOND" PUTT.

'Breakers'

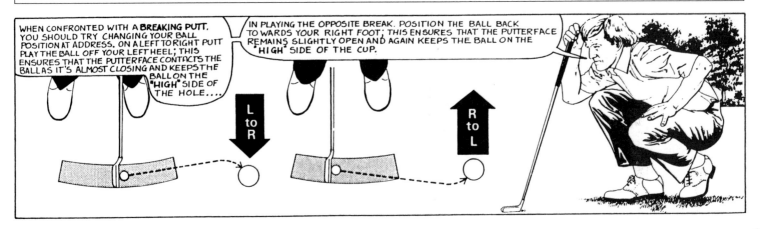

WHEN CONFRONTED WITH A **BREAKING PUTT**, YOU SHOULD TRY CHANGING YOUR BALL POSITION AT ADDRESS. ON A LEFT TO RIGHT PUTT PLAY THE BALL OFF YOUR LEFT HEEL; THIS ENSURES THAT THE PUTTERFACE CONTACTS THE BALL AS IT'S ALMOST CLOSING AND KEEPS THE BALL ON THE "HIGH" SIDE OF THE HOLE....

IN PLAYING THE OPPOSITE BREAK. POSITION THE BALL BACK TOWARDS YOUR RIGHT FOOT; THIS ENSURES THAT THE PUTTERFACE REMAINS SLIGHTLY OPEN AND AGAIN KEEPS THE BALL ON THE "HIGH" SIDE OF THE CUP.

L to R

R to L

45

Playing the Break

IT'S MY FEELING THAT MOST HANDICAP PLAYERS LEAVE PUTTS ON THE "AMATEUR SIDE" BECAUSE THEY DON'T FEEL COMFORTABLE GIVING THE HOLE AWAY AND HAVING TO TRUST THE SLOPE OF THE GREEN TO BRING IT BACK....

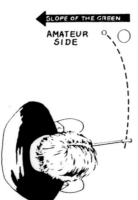

SLOPE OF THE GREEN

AMATEUR SIDE

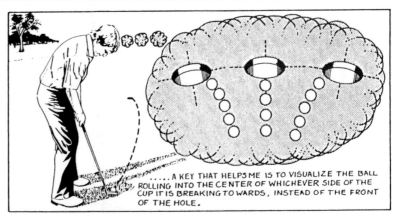

....A KEY THAT HELPS ME IS TO VISUALIZE THE BALL ROLLING INTO THE CENTER OF WHICHEVER SIDE OF THE CUP IT IS BREAKING TOWARDS, INSTEAD OF THE FRONT OF THE HOLE.

Don't underestimate overspin

A PUTT HIT A LITTLE OFF-TARGET OR OFF-SPEED WILL USUALLY STILL FIND ITS WAY INTO THE CUP, IF YOU IMPART **OVERSPIN** ON THE BALL.....

TO DO THIS, YOU MUST STRIKE A PUTT AS YOU SHOULD A DRIVE -- **ON THE UPSWING.** THIS TECHNIQUE SENDS THE BALL ROLLING END-OVER-END, THUS, CHANCES ARE, IF YOU HAVE READ THE PROPER BREAK INTO THE LINE, YOU'LL HOLE · OUT.....

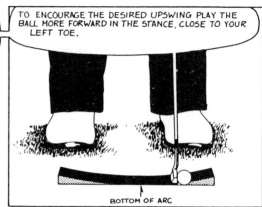

TO ENCOURAGE THE DESIRED UPSWING PLAY THE BALL MORE FORWARD IN THE STANCE, CLOSE TO YOUR LEFT TOE.

BOTTOM OF ARC

46

Beat the yips

THE PLAYER WHO STABS, OR **YIPS**, PUTTS, IS USUALLY ONE WHO LACKS CONFIDENCE IN HIS STROKE.
IF YOU CONTRACT A CASE OF THE YIPS FROM TIME TO TIME. PRACTICE HARD HOLING OUT VERY SHORT PUTTS. TRY TO MAKE 20 TWO FOOTERS IN A ROW, FOR EXAMPLE. BY PLAYING INVENTIVE LITTLE GAMES LIKE THIS, YOU WILL NOT ONLY FIRM UP YOUR STROKE, BUT YOU'LL BUILD UP THE POSITIVE ATTITUDE REQUIRED FOR POPPING THE BALL INTO THE HOLE CONSISTENTLY.

X ⓴

Cure the sway

THE MOST COMMON PUTTING ERROR A HIGH HANDICAPPER MAKES IS SWAYING OFF THE BALL.

TO ELIMINATE SWAYING DURING THE BACKSTROKE - A FAULT THAT LEADS TO AN OVERLY QUICK TEMPO —

PUT 60% OF YOUR WEIGHT ON YOUR LEFT FOOT AND LEAVE IT THERE WHILE YOU SWING THE PUTTER BLADE BACK AND THROUGH.

40%

60%

Reverse your thinking

THERE ARE SEVERAL GOOD PUTTING GRIPS. HOWEVER, THE ONE I PREFER TO ASSUME WHEN SETTING UP TO STROKE A PUTT IS THE REVERSE OVERLAP GRIP AS IT KEEPS THE HANDS AND WRISTS OUT OF THE STROKE.

I'VE ALWAYS PREFERRED TO MAKE A DEAD-HANDED, DEAD-WRISTED STROKE. THIS STROKE ALLOWS ME TO KEEP THE BLADE SQUARE TO THE HOLE IN THE HITTING AREA. AND THAT'S ONE OF THE MAJOR KEYS TO GOOD PUTTING.
THE REVERSE OVERLAP GRIP WILL ALSO HELP YOU QUIETEN YOUR HAND ACTION. TO ASSUME THIS HOLD GRIP NORMALLY WITH YOUR RIGHT HAND BUT DRAPE YOUR LEFT FOREFINGER OVER THE FIRST FOUR FINGERS OF YOUR RIGHT.

PUTTING

Fringe benefits

WHEN THE BALL RESTS JUST A FEW INCHES FROM THE EDGE OF THE FRINGE, YOU'LL USUALLY HAVE A RESTRICTED BACKSWING............

TO COMBAT THIS ON-COURSE PROBLEM I USE THE LEADING EDGE OF MY SAND IRON, WITH THE SAME SET-UP AS YOUR PUTTING ACTION. ADDRESS THE BALL AS IF YOU WERE GOING TO PUTT IT. PLACE THE LEADING EDGE OF THE SAND IRON ON THE TOP HALF OF THE BALL. THEN PLAY YOUR NORMAL STROKE. THE GRASS FROM THE FRINGE WILL NOT AFFECT THE CLUB'S SPEED AND THE BALL WILL ROLL LIKE A PUTT.

48

Maintain the triangle

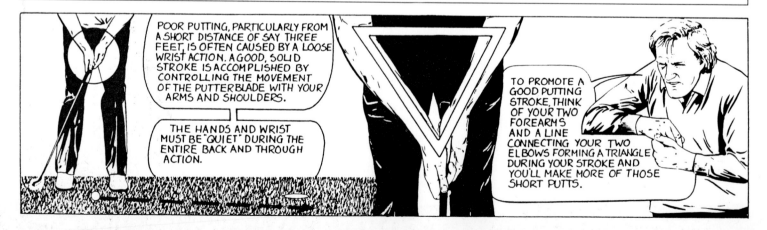

POOR PUTTING, PARTICULARLY FROM A SHORT DISTANCE OF SAY THREE FEET, IS OFTEN CAUSED BY A LOOSE WRIST ACTION. A GOOD, SOLID STROKE IS ACCOMPLISHED BY CONTROLLING THE MOVEMENT OF THE PUTTERBLADE WITH YOUR ARMS AND SHOULDERS.

THE HANDS AND WRIST MUST BE "QUIET" DURING THE ENTIRE BACK AND THROUGH ACTION.

TO PROMOTE A GOOD PUTTING STROKE, THINK OF YOUR TWO FOREARMS AND A LINE CONNECTING YOUR TWO ELBOWS FORMING A TRIANGLE DURING YOUR STROKE AND YOU'LL MAKE MORE OF THOSE SHORT PUTTS.

CHIPPING

CHIPPING

Chipping 1

NO

IF YOUR BIGGEST DRAWBACK IS HITTING CHIPSHOT EITHER WELL LEFT OR WELL RIGHT OF THE HOLE, AN OVERLY LOOSE "HANDSY" ACTION MAYBE TO BLAME.

ONE PROVEN KEY TO HITTING ON-LINE CHIPS IS TO SWING THE CLUB VIRTUALLY STRAIGHT BACK AND STRAIGHT THROUGH ALONG THE TARGET LINE.

TO HELP YOU TO ACCOMPLISH THIS GOAL, KEEP YOUR HANDS AND WRISTS QUIET IN THE BACK-SWING. THEN, AFTER STARTING DOWN, KEEP THE BACK OF YOUR LEFT HAND SQUARE TO THE HOLE IN THE HITTING AREA.

YES

Chipping 2

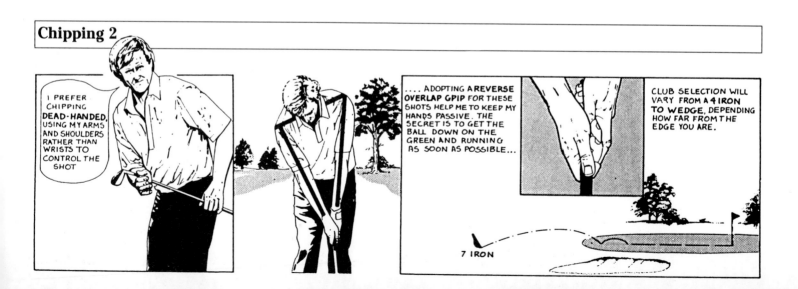

I PREFER CHIPPING **DEAD-HANDED,** USING MY ARMS AND SHOULDERS RATHER THAN WRISTS TO CONTROL THE SHOT

.... ADOPTING A **REVERSE OVERLAP GRIP** FOR THESE SHOTS HELP ME TO KEEP MY HANDS PASSIVE. THE SECRET IS TO GET THE BALL DOWN ON THE GREEN AND RUNNING AS SOON AS POSSIBLE...

CLUB SELECTION WILL VARY FROM A 4 IRON TO WEDGE, DEPENDING HOW FAR FROM THE EDGE YOU ARE.

7 IRON

EVEN MANY AVERAGE BALL STRIKERS SCORE WELL BECAUSE THEY HAVE EXCELLENT SHORT GAMES. MY ADVICE TO YOU IS THIS NO MATTER HOW WELL YOU SCORE. YOU CAN SCORE BETTER IF YOU DEVELOP A LEAK-PROOF CHIPPING GAME. THE GOLDEN RULES OF CHIPPING ARE....

1 CHOOSE A CLUB THAT YOU KNOW WILL CARRY THE FRINGE AND LAND THE BALL ON THE EDGE OF THE GREEN.

NO   YES

2. PICK A SPECIFIC SPOT ON THE GREEN TO LAND THE BALL.

3 VISUALIZE THE BALL HITTING THAT SPOT BEFORE YOU SWING.

4 TRY TO KEEP THE CLUBFACE PRETTY MUCH SQUARE TO YOUR BALL-TO-SPOT LINE ON THE BACKSWING.

51

The putt-chip

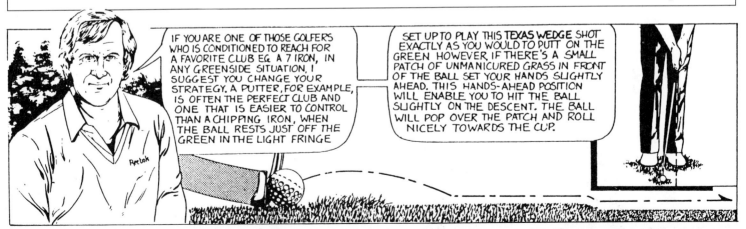

IF YOU ARE ONE OF THOSE GOLFERS WHO IS CONDITIONED TO REACH FOR A FAVORITE CLUB E.G. A 7 IRON, IN ANY GREENSIDE SITUATION, I SUGGEST YOU CHANGE YOUR STRATEGY. A PUTTER, FOR EXAMPLE, IS OFTEN THE PERFECT CLUB AND ONE THAT IS EASIER TO CONTROL THAN A CHIPPING IRON, WHEN THE BALL RESTS JUST OFF THE GREEN IN THE LIGHT FRINGE

SET UP TO PLAY THIS **TEXAS WEDGE** SHOT EXACTLY AS YOU WOULD TO PUTT ON THE GREEN HOWEVER IF THERE'S A SMALL PATCH OF UNMANICURED GRASS IN FRONT OF THE BALL SET YOUR HANDS SLIGHTLY AHEAD. THIS HANDS-AHEAD POSITION WILL ENABLE YOU TO HIT THE BALL SLIGHTLY ON THE DESCENT. THE BALL WILL POP OVER THE PATCH AND ROLL NICELY TOWARDS THE CUP.

CHIPPING

Hands first

PROBABLY, THE MOST COMMON FAULT ON CHIP SHOTS IS ALLOWING THE CLUBHEAD TO GET AHEAD OF THE HANDS BEFORE IMPACT. THE HANDS MUST LEAD THE CLUBHEAD INTO THE BALL FOR CRISP HITS.

ONE WAY OF DEVELOPING THIS MUST OF CHIPPING TECHNIQUE IS TO IMAGINE A LINE EXTENDING FROM YOUR CHIN TO THE BALL.....

BAD

ON THE DOWNSWING, MAKE YOUR HANDS BREAK THE LINE FIRST.

GOOD

HANDS FIRST

Topped short shots

CONSISTENTLY MIS-HITTING THE BALL AROUND THE GREENS WILL RUN YOUR SCORE UP FAST. IF YOU'RE FREQUENTLY TOPPING YOUR CHIPS, PITCHES AND SAND SHOTS, IT COULD BE BECAUSE YOU'RE LIFTING YOUR UPPER BODY DURING THE DOWNSWING.....

TO CURE THIS, TRY FLEXING YOUR KNEES A LITTLE MORE. IF YOU MAINTAIN THE FLEX THROUGHOUT THE SWING, YOU'LL HIT THE BALL SOLIDLY EVERY TIME.

WEDGE SHOTS

WEDGE SHOTS

Short wedges

THE 1/2 AND 3/4 WEDGE SHOT CAN BE EITHER A GREAT SHOT-SAVER, OR STROKE-WASTER. PLAYERS WHO FEAR THEM USUALLY HURRY THE SHOT, LEADING TO A QUICK SWING AND OFTEN RUINOUS RESULTS.

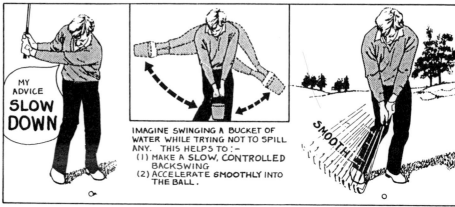

MY ADVICE SLOW DOWN

IMAGINE SWINGING A BUCKET OF WATER WHILE TRYING NOT TO SPILL ANY. THIS HELPS TO :-
(1) MAKE A SLOW, CONTROLLED BACKSWING
(2) ACCELERATE SMOOTHLY INTO THE BALL.

SMOOTH

Hitting the Half-wedge

A GOOD WAY TO DETERMINE HOW HARD YOU SHOULD SWING ON A LESS THAN FULL WEDGE SHOT IS TO BREAK THE BACKSWING DOWN INTO PARTS.....

SWING THE HANDS BACK TO ABOUT HIP LEVEL FOR A ONE-QUARTER SWING.

TO MIDWAY BETWEEN THE THE HIPS AND SHOULDERS FOR A HALF SWING

AND TO SHOULDER LEVEL FOR A THREE-QUARTER SWING. REMEMBER TO EMPHASIZE GOOD TEMPO AND ACCELERATION THROUGH THE BALL ON THESE SHOTS.

BUNKER SHOTS

BUNKER SHOTS

The explosion shot

I'VE LEARNED A LOT ABOUT GREENSIDE BUNKER PLAY FROM GREAT PLAYERS LIKE CHI CHI RODRIGUEZ AND GARY PLAYER

SET UP WITH AN OPEN STANCE AND A VERY OPEN FACE....

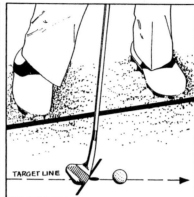

TARGET LINE

.... ADDRESS AN IMAGINARY SPOT ABOUT 1½" BEHIND THE BALL, PLAYING IT OFF YOUR LEFT HEEL. KNIFE THE BLADE INTO THE SPOT AND UNDER THE BALL, EXPLODING IT AND THE SAND IT LIES ON OUT OF THE TRAP.

Fairway bunker play

WHEN PLAYING FROM A FAIRWAY BUNKER, DIG IN JUST ENOUGH WITH YOUR FEET TO FORM A GOOD FOUNDATION, AND PLAY THE BALL IN THE CENTRE OF YOUR STANCE.

CHOKE UP ON THE CLUB AND MAKE A THREE-QUARTER SWING, CONCENTRATING ON KEEPING THE HANDS "UP" A FRACTION AS THEY SWEEP THROUGH THE HITTING AREA TO AVOID CATCHING ANY SAND BEFORE THE BALL

UP

NO

YES

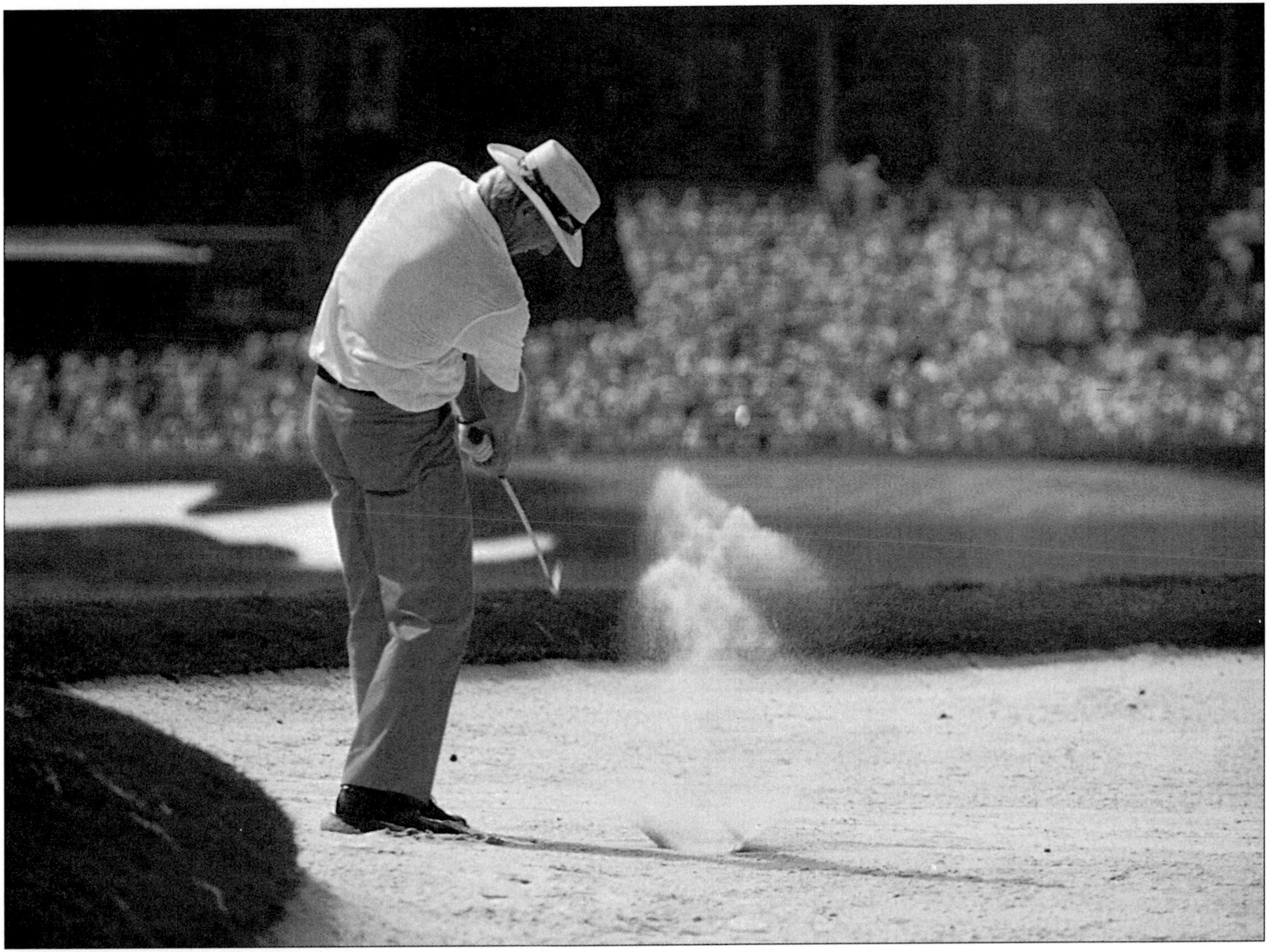

BUNKER SHOTS

Uphill bunker play

WHEN FACED WITH AN UPHILL BUNKER SHOT PLAY THE BALL IN THE CENTRE OF A NARROW BUT OPEN STANCE. USE A 'WEAK' GRIP. BE SURE YOUR CLUBFACE LOOKS DIRECTLY AT THE TARGET.

TARGET LINE

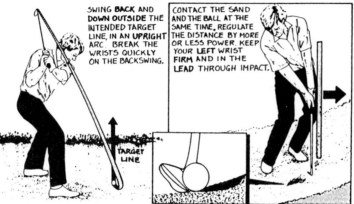

SWING **BACK** AND **DOWN OUTSIDE** THE INTENDED TARGET LINE, IN AN **UPRIGHT** ARC. BREAK THE WRISTS QUICKLY ON THE BACKSWING.

TARGET LINE

CONTACT THE SAND AND THE BALL AT THE SAME TIME. REGULATE THE DISTANCE BY MORE OR LESS POWER. KEEP YOUR **LEFT WRIST** **FIRM** AND IN THE **LEAD** THROUGH IMPACT.

SHAVE LITTLE SAND OUT FROM UNDER THE BALL. FINISH HIGH.

Brave the bunkers

PLUGGED BALLS IN THE SAND SCARE MANY PLAYERS. THE TRUTH IS, IT'S EASY TO RECOVER FROM SUCH LIES IF YOU :-

1. DIG YOUR FEET INTO THE SAND FOR STABLE FOOTING
2. CLOSE THE CLUBFACE EXAGGERATEDLY.
3. TAKE A FULL NORMAL SWING.

YOU'LL SEE, THE BALL WILL POP UP AND RUN QUICKLY, SO BE SURE TO PLAY THIS SHOT ONLY WHEN YOU HAVE PLENTY OF GREEN TO WORK WITH....

IF YOU DON'T HAVE A LOT OF GREEN, OPEN THE BLADE AS FLAT AS A PANCAKE AND BLAST THE SAND HARD.

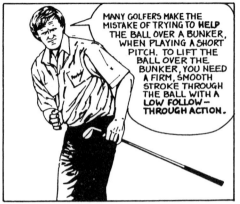

MANY GOLFERS MAKE THE MISTAKE OF TRYING TO HELP THE BALL OVER A BUNKER, WHEN PLAYING A SHORT PITCH. TO LIFT THE BALL OVER THE BUNKER, YOU NEED A FIRM, SMOOTH STROKE THROUGH THE BALL WITH A LOW FOLLOW-THROUGH ACTION.

IN FACT, SO LOW, THAT YOU SHOULD FEEL AS IF YOU ARE HITTING A VERY, VERY, LONG PUTT.

THINK OF PUTTING YOUR WEDGE SHOTS AND YOU'LL BEAT THE PITCH-OVER-BUNKER BLUES.

NO

YES

Money talks

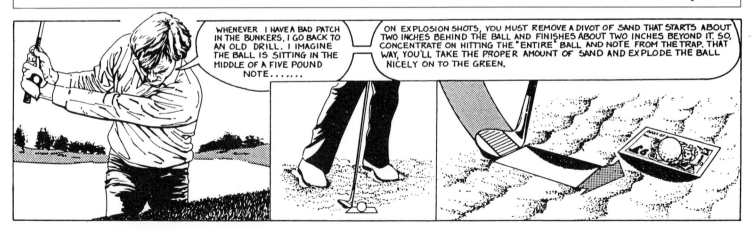

WHENEVER I HAVE A BAD PATCH IN THE BUNKERS, I GO BACK TO AN OLD DRILL. I IMAGINE THE BALL IS SITTING IN THE MIDDLE OF A FIVE POUND NOTE.......

ON EXPLOSION SHOTS, YOU MUST REMOVE A DIVOT OF SAND THAT STARTS ABOUT TWO INCHES BEHIND THE BALL AND FINISHES ABOUT TWO INCHES BEYOND IT. SO, CONCENTRATE ON HITTING THE "ENTIRE" BALL AND NOTE FROM THE TRAP. THAT WAY, YOU'LL TAKE THE PROPER AMOUNT OF SAND AND EXPLODE THE BALL NICELY ON TO THE GREEN.

BUNKER SHOTS

The long sand shot

I CONCEDE THAT THE 35-50 YARD SAND SHOT, TO A PIN CUT ON THE TOP TIER OF A GREEN, IS ONE OF THE TOUGHEST SHOTS IN GOLF.

NEVERTHELESS, YOU CAN LEARN TO MASTER THIS SHOT AND HIT THE BALL CLOSE TO THE HOLE IF YOU PLAY A PITCHING WEDGE AND SWING ON A FLATTER PLANE.

SAND IRON

PITCHING WEDGE

A PITCHING WEDGE IS LESS LOFTED THAN THE SAND IRON.

THEREFORE, WHEN SWINGING IT ON AN EXAGGERATED INSIDE-SQUARE – INSIDE PATH, THE BALL WILL ROLL ALL THE WAY TO THE HOLE ONCE IT LANDS ON THE GREENS LOWER LEVEL.

From the sand

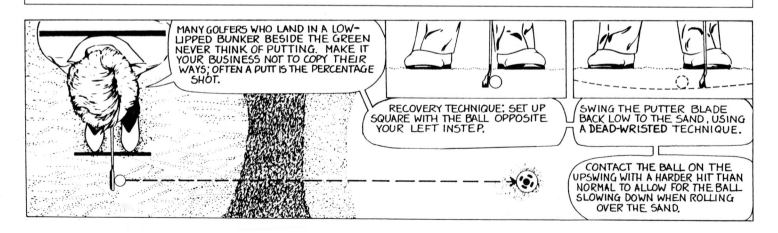

MANY GOLFERS WHO LAND IN A LOW-LIPPED BUNKER BESIDE THE GREEN NEVER THINK OF PUTTING. MAKE IT YOUR BUSINESS NOT TO COPY THEIR WAYS; OFTEN A PUTT IS THE PERCENTAGE SHOT.

RECOVERY TECHNIQUE: SET UP SQUARE WITH THE BALL OPPOSITE YOUR LEFT INSTEP.

SWING THE PUTTER BLADE BACK LOW TO THE SAND, USING A DEAD-WRISTED TECHNIQUE.

CONTACT THE BALL ON THE UPSWING WITH A HARDER HIT THAN NORMAL TO ALLOW FOR THE BALL SLOWING DOWN WHEN ROLLING OVER THE SAND.

Bunker practice

MANY GOLFERS ARE POOR SAND PLAYERS BECAUSE...

THEY DO NOT PLAN OUT A SHOT BEFORE STEPPING INTO A BUNKER. DO NOT MAKE THE SAME MISTAKE.

REHEARSE YOUR SHOT IN THE FOLLOWING MANNER........

1. STAND OUTSIDE THE BUNKER AND SELECT A SPOT IN THE GRASS TO REPRESENT THE BALL.

2. WITH A SAND WEDGE MAKE A WRISTY SWING, HITTING THE TURF 2 INCHES BEHIND THE SPOT YOU PICKED.

NOW YOU ARE READY !!!

2"

61

Simplify sand play

THE AVERAGE GOLFER HAS A TENDENCY TO PANIC WHEN HE FINDS HIS BALL IN A SAND BUNKER - EVEN IF IT IS SITTING UP.

BECAUSE HE FEARS THE BUNKER SHOTS, HE EITHER TRIES TO DIG THE BALL OUT OR PICK IT OUT. BOTH OF THOSE STRATEGIES ARE WRONG !

No

No

TO RECOVER WELL CONSISTENTLY FROM A GOOD LIE IN A BUNKER, YOU MUST SHAVE SOME SAND FROM UNDER THE BALL. SO SET UP **OPEN**, SWING THE CLUB UP **OUTSIDE** THE LINE, THEN **CUT** ACROSS THE BALL AND HIT TWO INCHES BEHIND IT COMING THROUGH.

2"

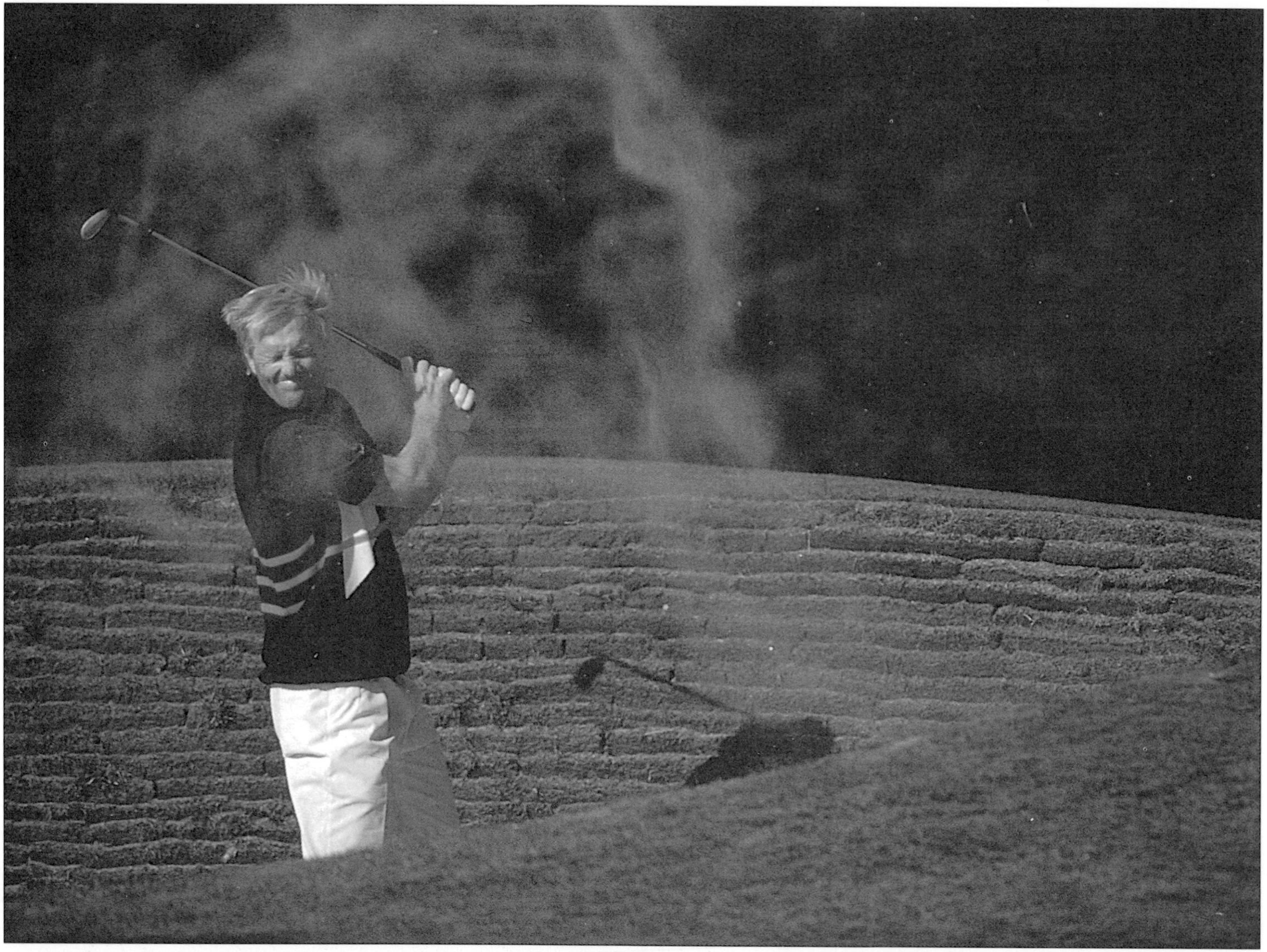

THE ROUGH

From the rough

HITTING A SOFT SHOT OUT OF LIGHT ROUGH IS EASY. HERE'S HOW TO DO IT.

ADDRESS: SET MORE OF YOUR WEIGHT ON YOUR RIGHT FOOT.

UPRIGHT

NORMAL

BACKSWING: MAKE AN EXAGGERATED UPRIGHT SWING.

BALL POSITION

DOWNSWING: SWING THE CLUB DOWN WITH YOUR HANDS AND ARMS AND KEEP YOUR HEAD BEHIND THE BALL UNTIL IMPACT.

THE SHOT WILL FLY ABOUT 10 YARDS FARTHER BECAUSE GRASS INTERVENES BETWEEN THE BALL AND THE CLUBFACE AT IMPACT, SO COMPENSATE BY HITTING ONE CLUB SHORTER THAN NORMAL.

Respect the rough

WHEN PLAYING OUT OF ROUGH, IT'S IMPORTANT TO RESPECT THE LIMITATIONS IT IMPOSES. LONG GRASS TENDS TO WRAP AROUND THE HOSAL, REDUCING CLUBHEAD SPEED AND CLOSING THE CLUBFACE....

BECAUSE OF THIS AVOID ATTEMPTING LONG IRONS FROM THE ROUGH AND INSTEAD TRY A 4 OR 5 WOOD. THE LARGER ROUNDED HEAD GLIDES THROUGH THE GRASS INSTEAD OF GETTING CAUGHT IN IT.

A rough pitch made easy

PLAYING A SHORT PITCH FROM GREENSIDE ROUGH ISN'T THAT DIFFICULT IF YOU USE THE PROPER TECHNIQUE...

TAKE A SAND WEDGE, OPEN THE CLUBFACE SLIGHTLY AND PLAY THE SHOT LIKE AN EXPLOSION FROM SAND...

USE A QUICK WRIST BREAK AND HIT ABOUT **3 INCHES** BEHIND THE BALL; SLIDING THE CLUB THROUGH THE GRASS AND UNDER THE BALL WITH YOUR RIGHT HAND...

THE SHOT WILL FLY HIGH AND LAND SOFTLY WITH LITTLE ROLL.

3 INCHES

Explosion from the rough

.... INSTEAD OF TAKING AN AGGRESSIVE STROKE WITH A PITCHING WEDGE, PLAY A SAND WEDGE AND PRETEND YOUR HITTING AN EXPLOSION FROM SAND. ALLOW THE BLADE TO CONTACT THE GRASS ABOUT AN INCH BEHIND THE BALL; THAT TECHNIQUE WILL POP THE BALL SOFTLY IN THE AIR, SO IT STOPS RELATIVELY QUICKLY NEXT TO THE FLAG.

WHEN THE BALL LIES IN WIRY GRASS BORDERING THE GREEN - U.S. OPEN TYPE ROUGH, AS I CALL IT - LEAVE THE PITCHING WEDGE IN THE BAG AND SWITCH YOUR STRAGEGY.....

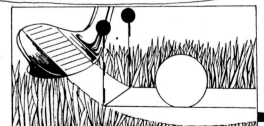

THE ROUGH

Use Cutspin

WHEN THE ROUGH IS LUSH AND LONG, HITTING THE BALL WITH SOFT FLIGHT, SO IT SITS DOWN PRETTY QUICKLY ON THE GREEN, IS QUITE DEMANDING...

...THE BEST WAY TO ACCOMPLISH THIS GOAL IS TO PUT SOME CUTTING ACTION ON THE BALL. HERE'S HOW:—

1. ASSUME AN OPEN STANCE, WITH MORE WEIGHT ON YOUR LEFT FOOT; 2. SWING THE CLUB BACK PURPOSELY OUTSIDE THE TARGET LINE AND ON AN EXTREMELY UPRIGHT PLANE;

TARGET LINE

TARGET LINE

3. SWING DOWN ACROSS THE BALL, HOLDING ON MORE TIGHTLY WITH YOUR LEFT HAND TO DELAY THE NORMAL HAND-RELEASING ACTION. NOW THE BALL WILL MOVE "QUIETLY" FROM LEFT TO RIGHT AND SIT DOWN SOFTLY.

Utility woods work!

WHEN CONFRONTED WITH A LONG SHOT FROM THICK ROUGH, DON'T AUTOMATICALLY REACH FOR A LONG IRON. THESE TYPES OF "STICKS" WILL ONLY TWIST AND TURN THROUGH IMPACT. YOU NEED SOMETHING THAT WILL PLOUGH THROUGH THE ROUGH. OPT FOR A "UTILITY" WOOD....

...A 5, 6, OR 7-WOOD THAT IS SOLE-WEIGHTED WILL ALLOW YOU TO KNOCK THE BALL A LONG WAY DOWN THE FAIRWAY WITH A LOT LESS EFFORT. SO, YOU'LL NATURALLY MAINTAIN THE GOOD TEMPO YOU NEED TO HIT THE BALL ACCURATELY TO YOUR TARGET.

IRON   WOOD

Softly softly

JUST BECAUSE THE BALL IS NESTLED IN THICK ROUGH AROUND THE GREEN, THAT DOESN'T MEAN YOU HAVE TO HIT HARD. IN FACT, THE BEST WAY TO EXTRACT THE BALL OUT OF THE FRINGE GRASS AND LAND IT SOFTLY ON THE GREEN IS 'NOT' TO GO ABOUT IT AGGRESSIVELY.

STEEP

SWING THE CLUB SLOWLY UP ON A STEEP PLANE, THEN, DROP THE CLUBHEAD A COUPLE OF INCHES BEHIND THE BALL, AS IN A SHORT SAND SHOT.

Shot over the tree

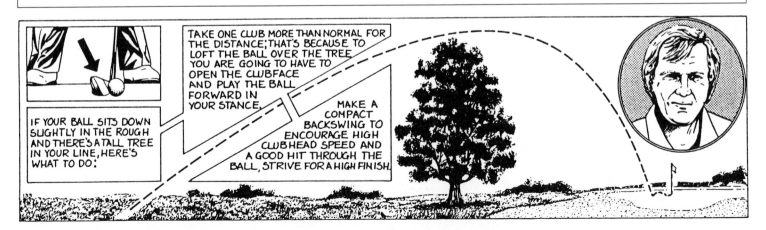

IF YOUR BALL SITS DOWN SLIGHTLY IN THE ROUGH AND THERE'S A TALL TREE IN YOUR LINE, HERE'S WHAT TO DO:

TAKE ONE CLUB MORE THAN NORMAL FOR THE DISTANCE; THAT'S BECAUSE TO LOFT THE BALL OVER THE TREE YOU ARE GOING TO HAVE TO OPEN THE CLUBFACE AND PLAY THE BALL FORWARD IN YOUR STANCE,

MAKE A COMPACT BACKSWING TO ENCOURAGE HIGH CLUBHEAD SPEED AND A GOOD HIT THROUGH THE BALL, STRIVE FOR A HIGH FINISH.

TACTICS

Think target

BEING "BALL-BOUND" LEADS TO A FROZEN TYPE OF SWINGING ACTION. THE PLAYER FAILS TO MAKE A FREE FLAILING ACTION THROUGH THE BALL BECAUSE HIS MUSCLES TIGHTENED......

.....TO ENCOURAGE RELAXATION AND AN EVENLY FLOWING SWING MOTION, THINK "TARGET", NOT BALL. THAT WAY YOU WON'T PECK AT THE BALL WITH THE CLUBFACE. YOU'LL SWING POWERFULLY THROUGH IT AND SEND IT FLYING AT YOUR TARGET.

70

Use an intermediate target

AS AN AID TO AIMING GET INTO THE HABIT OF USING AN INTERMEDIATE TARGET. BEFORE YOU STEP UP TO THE BALL, STAND BEHIND IT AND SIGHT DOWN THE TARGET LINE TO PICK OUT A SPOT ON THE LINE JUST A SHORT DISTANCE IN FRONT OF THE BALL..

THEN, AS YOU ADDRESS THE SHOT, SQUARE THE CLUBFACE TO THAT SPOT..

...AND THEN YOUR BODY TO THE CLUBFACE

WHEN FACED WITH A TEE SHOT DOWN AN EXTRA NARROW FAIRWAY TRY PLAYING THIS MENTAL TRICK. IMAGINE A LARGE TARGET ON THE FAIRWAY, 20 YARDS IN FRONT OF YOUR TEEING SPOT. THEN TRY TO HIT OVER IT......

IF YOU NATURALLY HIT A DRAW OR A FADE, IMAGINE THE TARGET ON THE SIDE WHERE YOUR BALL STARTS ITS FLIGHT.

THIS STRATEGY MAY SOUND SILLY, BUT I GUARANTEE IT WILL GIVE YOU BETTER IMAGERY AT ADDRESS, AND THAT'S ONE KEY TO PERFECTLY PLACING TEE SHOTS ON THE FAIRWAY.

71

Soft flight

PRACTICING HITTING SHOTS WITH YOUR FEET TOGETHER WILL CONDITION YOU TO SWING THE CLUB WITH YOUR ARMS, INSTEAD OF YOUR BODY (I.E COMING OVER THE TOP WITH YOUR RIGHT SHOULDER), AS SO MANY CLUB-LEVEL PLAYERS DO.

IF YOUR SHORT-MEDIUM IRON SHOTS ARE FLYING LOW AND BOUNDING OVER THE GREEN, YOU'RE PROBABLY NOT MAKING A NICE FLOWING SWING WITH THE ARMS.

START WITH A VERY SHORT SWING AND PROGRESS TO LONGER SWINGS. ONCE YOUR SHOTS BEGIN FLYING UPWARDS WITH SOFT FLIGHT, STAND NORMALLY AND GROOVE A GOOD THING.

TACTICS

Think finish first

PLAYERS WHO TRY TO POUND THE BALL OUT OF SIGHT USUALLY CAUSE THEIR MUSCLES TO TIGHTEN, THUS THEIR FOLLOW-THROUGH IS ABBREVIATED. IF THIS IS THE CASE WITH YOUR SWING, YOU PROBABLY END UP HITTING THE BALL SHORT, NOT LONG....

LONG

SHORT

TO ENCOURAGE A STRONG SWING ACTION TRY THINKING OF THE FINISH AS YOU ASSUME YOUR ADDRESS POSITION; THIS MENTAL IMAGE WILL ENCOURAGE AN UNINHIBITED SWING WITH MAXIMUM CLUBHEAD SPEED IN THE IMPACT ZONE.

Don't quit

NO MATTER WHAT CLUB YOU ARE PLAYING "QUITTING" ON THE SHOT IS FATAL. EVEN ON SHORT PITCHES AND CHIPS YOU SHOULD CONCENTRATE ON ACCELERATING THROUGH THE BALL, TO THE TARGET.......

ONE SURE WAY TO ENSURE THIS PROPER FOLLOW-THROUGH ACTION IS TO LET YOUR HANDS STRETCH OUT TOWARD THE PIN AS YOU COME THROUGH THE BALL.....

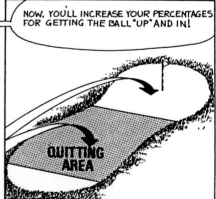

NOW, YOU'LL INCREASE YOUR PERCENTAGES FOR GETTING THE BALL "UP" AND IN!

QUITTING AREA

Move the shot

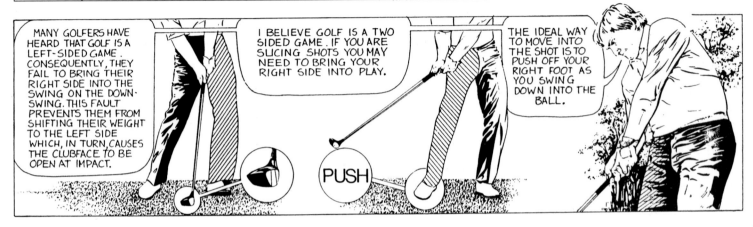

MANY GOLFERS HAVE HEARD THAT GOLF IS A LEFT-SIDED GAME. CONSEQUENTLY, THEY FAIL TO BRING THEIR RIGHT SIDE INTO THE SWING ON THE DOWN-SWING. THIS FAULT PREVENTS THEM FROM SHIFTING THEIR WEIGHT TO THE LEFT SIDE WHICH, IN TURN, CAUSES THE CLUBFACE TO BE OPEN AT IMPACT.

I BELIEVE GOLF IS A TWO SIDED GAME. IF YOU ARE SLICING SHOTS YOU MAY NEED TO BRING YOUR RIGHT SIDE INTO PLAY.

PUSH

THE IDEAL WAY TO MOVE INTO THE SHOT IS TO PUSH OFF YOUR RIGHT FOOT AS YOU SWING DOWN INTO THE BALL.

73

Long Iron lesson

THE PLAYER WHO USUALLY HITS LONG IRON SHOTS STRAIGHT, BUT SHORT OF THE GREEN, IS ONE WHO TRIES TO SCOOP THE BALL IN THE AIR.
WHEN YOU TRY TO HELP THE BALL IN THE AIR, YOU WRONGLY LEAVE MOST OF YOUR WEIGHT ON YOUR RIGHT FOOT AT IMPACT. THIS SWING FAULT CAUSES YOU TO HIT UP AND UNDER THE BALL TOO MUCH THUS IT FLIES HIGHER THAN NORMAL AND NOT AS FAR.

YOUR LESSON: KEY ON SWINGING THE CLUB THROUGH WITH YOUR HANDS AND ARMS AND LET THE NATURAL LOFT BUILT INTO THE CLUB'S FACE LIFT THE BALL UP.

TACTICS

Fairway woods

MANY CLUB PLAYERS HIT FAIRWAY WOODS FAT BECAUSE THEY PLAY THE BALL TOO CLOSE TO THE MID-POINT IN THEIR STANCE, WHEN IT SHOULD BE POSITIONED ONLY SLIGHTLY BEHIND THE LEFT HEEL.

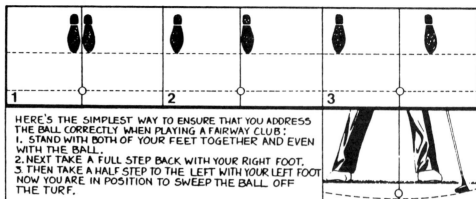

HERE'S THE SIMPLEST WAY TO ENSURE THAT YOU ADDRESS THE BALL CORRECTLY WHEN PLAYING A FAIRWAY CLUB:
1. STAND WITH BOTH OF YOUR FEET TOGETHER AND EVEN WITH THE BALL.
2. NEXT TAKE A FULL STEP BACK WITH YOUR RIGHT FOOT.
3. THEN TAKE A HALF STEP TO THE LEFT WITH YOUR LEFT FOOT NOW YOU ARE IN POSITION TO SWEEP THE BALL OFF THE TURF.

The Short Uphill

LET'S SAY YOUR BALL SITS SNUGLY IN A GRASSY UPHILL SLOPE BY THE GREEN. HERE ARE SOME SECRETS FOR HITTING THE BALL CLOSE TO THE HOLE.
ADDRESS: PLAY THE BALL OFF YOUR LEFT INSTEP, SET UP SQUARE AND LEAN YOUR WEIGHT HEAVILY INTO YOUR LEFT SIDE, CLOSE THE CLUBFACE A BIT TO COMPENSATE FOR IT OPENING AT IMPACT.

BACKSWING: SWING THE CLUB BACK TO KNEE HEIGHT KEEPING YOUR WRISTS FIRM AND WEIGHT ON YOUR LEFT.
DOWNSWING: PULL THE CLUB DOWN GENTLY INTO THE BALL KEEPING YOUR WRISTS UNCOCKED.

WIND SHOTS

WIND SHOTS

Learn the Low Punch

TO HIT A LOW BORING SHOT INTO HEAVY WIND OR UNDER TREE LIMBS, PLAY THE BALL BACK IN YOUR STANCE AND SET YOUR HANDS WELL AHEAD OF IT TO DELOFT THE CLUBFACE....

ASSUMING A SLIGHTLY OPEN STANCE, MAKE A NORMAL SWING, PULLING YOUR HANDS DOWN FIRMLY INTO THE BACK OF THE BALL...

PULL

THE RESULTING SHOT WILL FLY LOW AND HARD WITH LITTLE BACKSPIN, SO ALLOW FOR SOME ROLL.

Allow for the wind

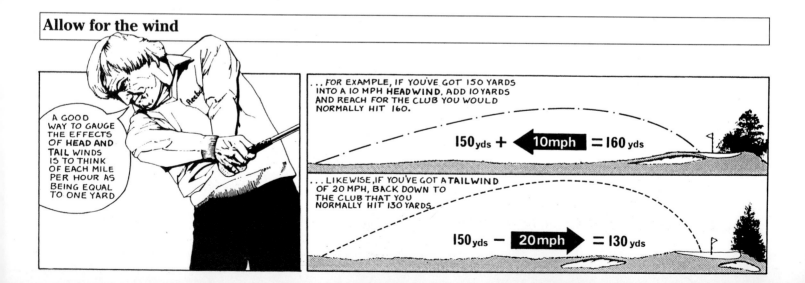

A GOOD WAY TO GAUGE THE EFFECTS OF HEAD AND TAIL WINDS IS TO THINK OF EACH MILE PER HOUR AS BEING EQUAL TO ONE YARD

...FOR EXAMPLE, IF YOU'VE GOT 150 YARDS INTO A 10 MPH HEADWIND, ADD 10 YARDS AND REACH FOR THE CLUB YOU WOULD NORMALLY HIT 160.

$$150_{yds} + \blacktriangleleft 10mph = 160_{yds}$$

...LIKEWISE, IF YOU'VE GOT A TAILWIND OF 20 MPH, BACK DOWN TO THE CLUB THAT YOU NORMALLY HIT 130 YARDS.

$$150_{yds} - 20mph \blacktriangleright = 130_{yds}$$

Winning in the wind

IF YOUR IRONS SHOTS SOAR TOO HIGH INTO THE WIND AND YOU LOSE DISTANCE, TRY DOING WHAT I DO: TAKE TWO MORE CLUBS AND CHOKE DOWN ON THE HANDLE FOR CONTROL......

THEN, KEEPING YOUR WRISTS "QUIET" SWING SLOWLY BACK TO THE THREE-QUARTER POSITION. ON THE WAY DOWN, KEY ON A STRONG WEIGHT SHIFT TO THE LEFT SIDE.....

..AND MOST IMPORTANTLY, LET YOUR HANDS LEAD THE CLUB THROUGH IMPACT. NOW, YOUR SHOTS WILL POWERFULLY PIERCE THE WIND.

77

The value of a good short game

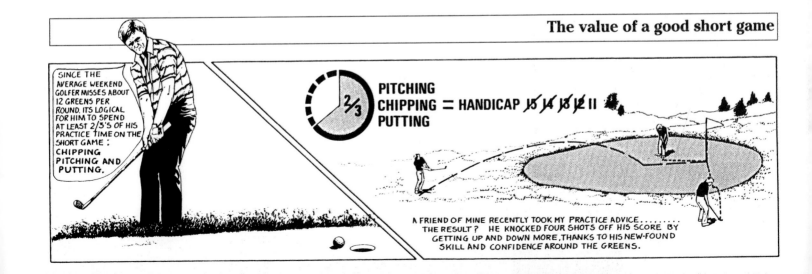

SINCE THE AVERAGE WEEKEND GOLFER MISSES ABOUT 12 GREENS PER ROUND, ITS LOGICAL FOR HIM TO SPEND AT LEAST 2/3'S OF HIS PRACTICE TIME ON THE SHORT GAME: CHIPPING PITCHING AND PUTTING.

2/3
PITCHING
CHIPPING = HANDICAP 15 14 13 12 11
PUTTING

A FRIEND OF MINE RECENTLY TOOK MY PRACTICE ADVICE......... THE RESULT? HE KNOCKED FOUR SHOTS OFF HIS SCORE BY GETTING UP AND DOWN MORE, THANKS TO HIS NEW-FOUND SKILL AND CONFIDENCE AROUND THE GREENS.

WIND SHOTS

Left side leads

WITH REGARDS TO THE SHORT GAME, MANY GOLFERS SHARE ONE PROBLEM: TRYING TO STEER THE BALL TO THE HOLE BY DRASTICALLY MOVING THEIR BODY. THIS SWING FAULT RESULTS IN EITHER A POORLY PULLED OR PUSHED SHOT.....

I LEARNED EARLY ON THAT YOU DON'T HAVE TO STEER THE BALL TO THE HOLE. TO HOLD THE CLUBFACE SQUARE TO THE TARGET YOU MUST PERMIT YOU LEFT ARM AND HAND TO BE DOMINANT THROUGH IMPACT...

TO ENABLE YOU TO GET THE FEEL OF A LEFT-SIDED LEAD, IMAGINE YOU ARE BACKHANDING YOUR WEDGE SHOTS WITH THE BACK OF THE LEFT HAND REMAINING PERPENDICULAR TO THE TARGET THROUGH THE HIT-ZONE AND INTO THE FOLLOW-THROUGH.

Tee it high

IF YOU LOSE VITAL DISTANCE ON YOUR TEE SHOTS WHEN HITTING INTO THE WIND, YOU MAY NOT HAVE THE BALL TEED HIGH ENOUGH.

THIS ADVICE MAY SURPRISE YOU HOWEVER. TEEING UP SO THAT SLIGHTLY MORE THAN HALF THE BALL IS ABOVE THE TOP OF THE CLUBFACE PROMOTES THE FLATTISH SWING PLANE THAT'S REQUIRED FOR PRODUCING A LOW DRIVE THAT ACTS LIKE A DART IN THE WIND.

NORMAL

FLATTER

Solid tee-shots

MANY AVERAGE GOLFERS HIT WEAK DRIVES BECAUSE THEY USE AN OVERLY "HANDSY" TECHNIQUE. PLAYERS WHO SWING THIS WAY PICK THE CLUB UP ON A STEEP PLANE AND CHOP DOWN ON THE BALL. THEREFORE, THE CLUB FAILS TO HIT THE BALL SQUARLY AND SOLIDLY.

TO TAP INTO YOUR NATURAL POWER SOURCE AND PROMOTE GOOD CLUBFACE-TO-BALL CONTACT DRIVE BOTH YOUR KNEES AT THE TARGET AT THE START OF YOUR DOWNSWING.

DON'T WORRY YOUR HANDS WILL FOLLOW YOUR LOWER BODY.

Through the gap for power

IF YOUR DRIVES LACK "OOMPH" YOU'RE PROBABLY NOT HITTING THE BALL WITH THE SWEETSPOT OF CLUBFACE AT IMPACT.....

THE CHANCES ARE YOU ARE SWINGING ACROSS THE TARGET LINE, RATHER THAN DOWN IT, IN THE IMPACT ZONE.....

TO ENSURE THAT YOU MAKE CLEAN CONTACT, TRY THIS DRILL IN PRACTICE. PLACE ONE TEE A HALF-INCH FROM THE HEEL OF THE DRIVER'S HEAD AND ANOTHER, THE SAME DISTANCE FROM THE TOE. NOW WORK HARD TO CONSISTENTLY GROOVE THE RIGHT PATH OF SWING BY HITTING THROUGH THE GAP OF TEES WITHOUT CONTACTING EITHER OF THEM.

POSITIONING

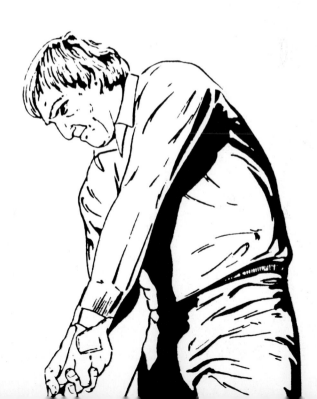

POSITIONING

Anti-sway set up

IF YOU ARE ONE OF THOSE GOLFERS WHO SWAYS OFF THE BALL ON THE BACKSWING, YOU'RE PROBABLY ARE ALSO ONE OF THOSE GOLFERS WHO MISSES THE FAIRWAYS AND GREENS.

TO PREVENT THE SWAY, POINT THE TOES OF YOUR RIGHT FOOT PERPENDICULAR TO THE TARGET LINE INSTEAD OF FANNING THEM OUTWARDS.

THIS RIGHT FOOT POSITION WILL SERVE AS A BACKSTOP TO COIL AGAINST THEREBY ALLOWING YOU TO COIL FULLY BEHIND THE BALL ON THE BACKSWING.

NO

YES

Stop the sway

GOLFERS WHO ROCK, OR "SWAY" THEIR BODY OFF THE BALL DURING THE BACKSWING ARE DESTINED TO HIT MISGUIDED SHOTS. THE REASON: FROM A "SWAY POSITION" IT'S VERY DIFFICULT TO TIME THE DOWNSWING THE RESULT IS USUALLY A WEAK SLICE.
TO CURE THE SWAY, IMAGINE THERE IS A STAKE PLANTED IN THE GROUND CLOSE TO YOUR RIGHT THIGH. NOW AS YOU TURN ON THE BACKSWING YOU'LL TEND TO COIL YOUR RIGHT HIP IN A CLOCKWISE DIRECTION AND NOT KNOCK INTO THE IMAGINARY STAKE.

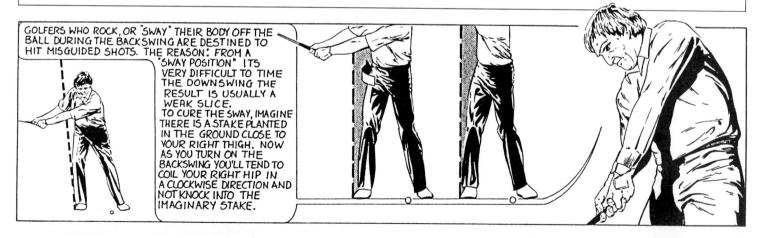

In the slot

BAD SLICES USUALLY RESULT WHEN THE CLUBFACE COMES INTO THE BALL FROM THE OUTSIDE. THIS OUT-TO-IN SWING PATH OFTEN CAN BE TRACED TO A JUTTING OUTWARD OF THE RIGHT SHOULDER EARLY IN THE DOWN-SWING........

TO CURE THIS FAULT, START YOUR DOWN-SWING WITH YOUR LOWER BODY AND DROP YOUR HANDS INTO THE HITTING **SLOT** AT ABOUT WAIST LEVEL. THAT WAY, YOUR RIGHT SHOULDER WILL STAY **CALM** AND THE CLUB WILL AUTOMATICALLY COME PROPERLY INTO THE BALL FROM THE **INSIDE**.

Be square

MANY GOLFERS MAKE THE MISTAKE OF AIMING THEIR LEFT SHOULDER BLADE AT THE TARGET. THIS FAULT FORCES THE SHOULDERS INTO AN EXAGGERATED CLOSED POSITION THEREBY PREVENTING A CORRECT INSIDE-SQUARE-INSIDE SWING PATH. THE RESULT: A BADLY HIT SHOT THAT FLIES OFF TARGET.

TO ENSURE YOU MAKE A SOUND SWING AND HIT THE BALL DEAD TO YOUR TARGET YOU SHOULD SET UP **SQUARE**. IN OTHER WORDS, YOUR LEFT SHOULDER SHOULD POINT SLIGHTLY LEFT OF YOUR TARGET LINE, AS SHOULD YOUR FEET KNEES AND HIPS. NOW, YOU'RE READY TO HIT A GREAT SHOT.

POSITIONING

Pull the pulley

TOO MANY PLAYERS IN TRYING TO FINESSE WEDGE SHOTS GET **LAZY**; THEIR SWINGS ARE OVERLY LOOSE, WITH SLOPPY WRIST ACTION THROUGH THE BALL...

LAZY

TO ENCOURAGE THE PROPER SWINGING ACTION THINK OF PULLING DOWN ON A PULLEY DURING THE DOWNSWING. THAT WAY, YOU'LL HIT FIRMLY THROUGH THE SHORT SHOTS WITH YOUR LEFT ARM AND HAND NICELY IN CONTROL. THEREFORE, YOU'LL ALWAYS GET **UP** AND HIT THOSE SHORT SHOTS ON THE MONEY, TOO.

Sqaure your set up

FOR SOME REASON, CLUB-LEVEL GOLFERS THINK THERE IS SOMETHING WRONG WITH THEIR SWING IF THEY SLICE THE BALL. ALTHOUGH A TECHNICAL BACKSWING OR DOWNSWING FAULT WOULD OBVIOUSLY CAUSE A SEVERE LEFT-TO-RIGHT SHOT, VERY OFTEN THE ROOT CAUSE OF THE SLICE CAN BE TRACED TO A BAD SETUP.

WRONG

IF YOU'RE SLICING CHECK YOUR ADDRESS. MAKE SURE THAT YOUR BENT KNEES, HIPS, AND SHOULDERS DON'T POINT LEFT OF THE TARGET BECAUSE THIS ADDRESS CAUSES YOU TO CUT ACROSS THE BALL AT IMPACT. FOR SOLID ACCURATE SHOTS, SET YOUR BODY PARALLEL OR "SQUARE" TO YOUR TARGET.

Ken Lewis

Straightening the Slice

MOST HIGH HANDICAPPERS I KNOW SUFFER FROM A **SLICE**, WHICH ROBS THEM OF BOTH **DISTANCE** AND **ACCURACY**.

THEIR PROBLEM OFTEN LIES IN EITHER THEIR **GRIP**, **ALIGNMENT**; OR A COMBINATION OF BOTH.

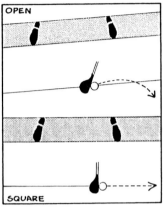

OPEN

SQUARE

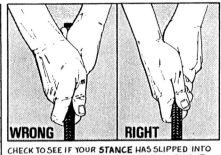

WRONG   RIGHT

CHECK TO SEE IF YOUR **STANCE** HAS SLIPPED INTO AN OPEN POSITION WITHOUT YOUR REALIZING IT. ALSO, TRY A **STRONGER GRIP** POSITION. EXPERIMENT BY TURNING YOUR HANDS **CLOCKWISE** GRADUALLY UNTIL YOUR SHOTS START STRAIGHTENING OUT.

Watch your divots

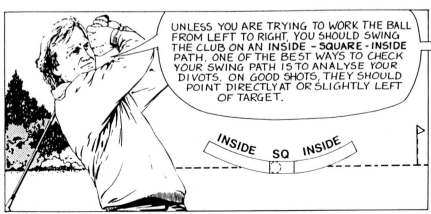

UNLESS YOU ARE TRYING TO WORK THE BALL FROM LEFT TO RIGHT, YOU SHOULD SWING THE CLUB ON AN INSIDE – SQUARE – INSIDE PATH. ONE OF THE BEST WAYS TO CHECK YOUR SWING PATH IS TO ANALYSE YOUR DIVOTS. ON GOOD SHOTS, THEY SHOULD POINT DIRECTLY AT OR SLIGHTLY LEFT OF TARGET.

INSIDE   SQ   INSIDE

IF YOUR DIVOTS POINT RIGHT OF TARGET YOU ARE PROBABLY SWINGING TOO MUCH FROM IN-TO-OUT

IF YOUR DIVOTS POINT WELL LEFT OF TARGET, YOU ARE SWINGING FAULTILY FROM OUT-TO-IN.

Cure your reverse pivot

IF YOU HIT HIGH, WEAK WILD SLICES YOU PROBABLY REVERSE PIVOT.

NO

ON THE BACKSWING YOU LEAVE YOUR WEIGHT ON YOUR LEFT FOOT, INSTEAD OF CORRECTLY SHIFTING IT TO YOUR RIGHT. WHEN YOU COMMIT THIS FAULT WEIGHT SHIFTS TO YOUR RIGHT FOOT ON THE DOWNSWING AND STAYS THERE AT IMPACT.

YES

NO

YES

YOUR WEIGHT SHOULD BE ON THE OUTSIDE OF YOUR LEFT FOOT AT IMPACT TO CURE THIS COMMON FAULT AND TO PROMOTE A GOOD WEIGHT SHIFT. ROTATE YOUR LEFT KNEE INWARDS AND ROTATE YOUR RIGHT HIP IN A CLOCKWISE DIRECTION ON THE BACKSWING.

86

Right side release

IF IN THE FINISH OF YOUR SWING, A LOT OF WEIGHT REMAINS ON YOUR RIGHT FOOT, THEN YOUR SUFFERING FROM A VERY COMMON FAULT · FAILING TO RELEASE YOUR RIGHT LEG FULLY ON THE DOWNSWING. WITH A STIFF RIGHT LEG, YOU LOSE A GREAT AMOUNT OF POWER BECAUSE YOU HAVEN'T PUT YOUR FULL WEIGHT BEHIND THE BALL AT IMPACT......

SO, ONCE YOUR LEFT SIDE LEADS YOU TARGETWARD, THINK OF TURNING THAT RIGHT KNEE IN THE SAME DIRECTION; AND DRIVE IT UNTIL ONLY YOUR RIGHT TOE REMAINS ON THE GROUND.

THIS IS A FOOL-PROOF WAY TO GUARANTEE STRAIGHT, SOLID TEE SHOTS.

Work your elbow

Get on the ball

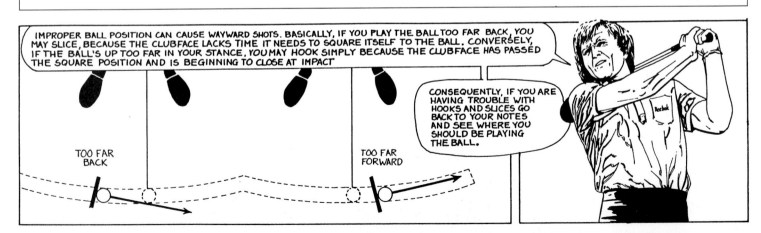

POSITIONING

The High Shot

MANY AMATEURS NAIVELY THINK THAT THEY HAVE TO MAKE ADJUSTMENTS TO THEIR TECHNIQUE TO HIT A HIGH SHOT

THAT'S NOT TRUE; ALL YOU NEED TO DO IS MOVE THE BALL FORWARD A COUPLE OF INCHES OR SO IN YOUR STANCE. MOVING THE BALL UP INCREASES THE EFFECTIVE LOFT OF THE CLUB, ENABLING YOU TO HIT THE BALL HIGH OVER TREES.

Play smart

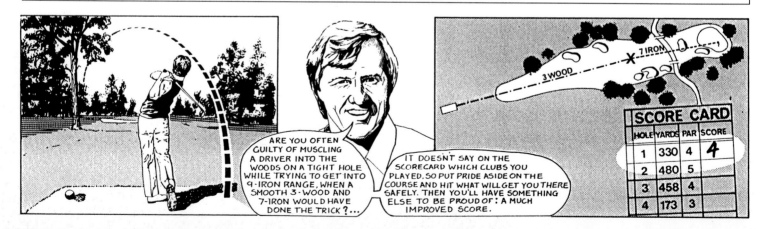

ARE YOU OFTEN GUILTY OF MUSCLING A DRIVER INTO THE WOODS ON A TIGHT HOLE WHILE TRYING TO GET INTO 9-IRON RANGE, WHEN A SMOOTH 3-WOOD AND 7-IRON WOULD HAVE DONE THE TRICK?...

IT DOESN'T SAY ON THE SCORECARD WHICH CLUBS YOU PLAYED, SO PUT PRIDE ASIDE ON THE COURSE AND HIT WHAT WILL GET YOU THERE SAFELY. THEN YOU'LL HAVE SOMETHING ELSE TO BE PROUD OF: A MUCH IMPROVED SCORE.

7 IRON

3 WOOD

SCORE CARD			
HOLE	YARDS	PAR	SCORE
1	330	4	4
2	480	5	
3	458	4	
4	173	3	

PROBLEMS

PROBLEMS

Bend your left arm

HAVING PLAYED IN NUMEROUS PRO AM TOURNAMENTS AROUND THE WORLD I THINK I KNOW THE SWING HABITS OF GOLFERS PRETTY WELL. ONE OF THE MOST COMMON FAULTS I SEE THE AVERAGE GOLFER MAKE HAS TO DO WITH THE NATURE OF HIS BACKSWING. HE IS TENSE, THEREFORE HIS BACKSWING IS SHORT. THE REASON IS HE TRIES TO KEEP HIS LEFT ARM STIFF.

IF YOU TENSE UP, SWING BACK SHORT OF THE PARALLEL POSITION AT THE TOP AND HIT THE BALL WEARILY, ALLOW YOUR LEFT ARM TO BEND SLIGHTLY ON THE BACKSWING.

Hands out

ON SHORT PITCH AND RUN SHOTS, IT'S BEST TO CUT OUT THE **FREQUENCIES** IN THE HANDS AND WRISTS. TOO MUCH ACTION IN THE HANDS AND WRISTS MAKES GAUGING DISTANCE TOUGH,....

....SO, (1) SELECT A SEVEN IRON. (2) SELECT A SPOT TO LAND AND (3) BE SELECT ABOUT YOUR TECHNIQUE. INSTEAD OF HITTING A **HANDSY** SHOT, REDUCE THE NUMBER OF MOVING PARTS IN YOUR SWING BY ALLOWING YOUR ARMS TO SWING THE CLUB BACK AND THROUGH, VIRTUALLY IN A PENDULUM-LIKE FASHION.

WRONG

7 IRON

RIGHT

Point your knees

TO WAKE UP A PAIR OF **DEAD LEGS** AND INCORPORATE THE ACTION OF THE LOWER BODY INTO YOUR SWING, THINK OF **POINTING** YOUR KNEES TO THE LEFT AS YOU MAKE YOUR DOWN SWING.

DOING THIS FORCES YOU TO SHIFT YOUR WEIGHT AGGRESSIVELY, RESULTING IN MORE POWER THROUGH THE BALL AND MORE DISTANCE ON YOUR SHOTS.

Why the Y?

ONE OF MY KEYS FOR HITTING GOOD GREENSIDE SHOTS IS MAINTAINING THE Y FORMED BY MY ARMS, HANDS, AND SHOULDERS THROUGHOUT THE SWING......

IF YOU TEND TO DRASTICALLY BREAK YOUR WRISTS AND DESTROY THE Y TRY IMAGINING THAT THE BODY PARTS THAT FORM THIS CRITICAL LETTER ARE CEMENTED TOGETHER AND MOVE IN ONE-PIECE WHILE YOUR LOWER BODY REMAINS RELATIVELY QUIET.

PROBLEMS

Anti-freeze

FREEZING OVER THE BALL IS A COMMON FAULT OF THE HIGH HANDICAPPER.

THE TYPICAL PLAYER STANDS RIGIDLY STILL OVER THE BALL FOR SO LONG THAT, WHEN THE TIME COMES TO SWING HE TENSES UP.

1

THE BEST WAY TO MAKE THE SWING FLOW IS TO ALLOW THE SET UP TO FLOW. DO ALL OF YOUR SIZING UP OF THE SHOT BEFORE YOU SET UP TO KNOW WHAT TYPE OF SHOT YOU WANT TO HIT AND WHERE YOU WANT THE BALL TO LAND THEN:

① TAKE YOUR ADDRESS POSITION QUICKLY.
② STARE AT THE TARGET.
③ WAGGLE THE CLUB AND GO.

2

3

'Dews' and don'ts

HERE'S SOME ADVICE FOR YOU GOLFING EARLY BIRDS WHO HAVE TROUBLE TWO PUTTING FROM OVER 20 FEET, BECAUSE MORNING DEW COVERS THE GREENS. YOU MUST STROKE THE BALL MORE FIRMLY TO ENSURE THAT THE BALL GETS THROUGH THE MOISTURE AND UP TO THE HOLE.....

FIRM

IN FIGURING THE LINE, YOU MUST HALF THE BREAKING DISTANCE BECAUSE THE DEW PREVENTS THE BALL FROM FOLLOWING THE NATURAL CONTOURS OF THE GREEN.

DEW LINE
DRY LINE

One hole journeys

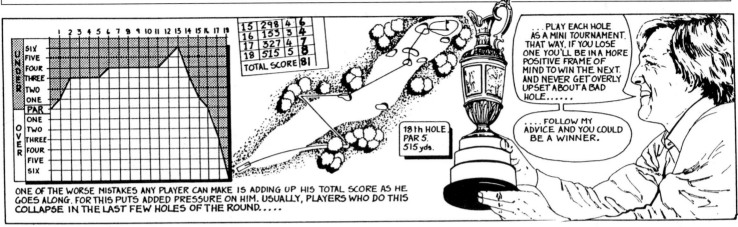

ONE OF THE WORSE MISTAKES ANY PLAYER CAN MAKE IS ADDING UP HIS TOTAL SCORE AS HE GOES ALONG. FOR THIS PUTS ADDED PRESSURE ON HIM. USUALLY, PLAYERS WHO DO THIS COLLAPSE IN THE LAST FEW HOLES OF THE ROUND.....

93

Out of a divot hole

PROBLEMS

Watch the ball

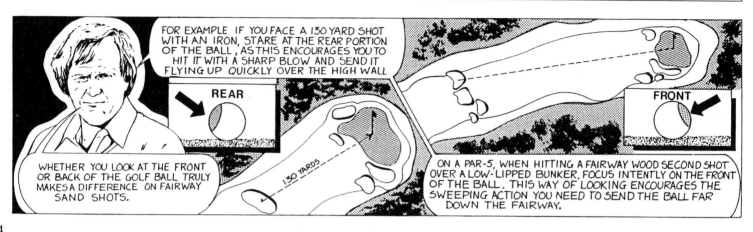

FOR EXAMPLE IF YOU FACE A 130 YARD SHOT WITH AN IRON, STARE AT THE REAR PORTION OF THE BALL, AS THIS ENCOURAGES YOU TO HIT IT WITH A SHARP BLOW AND SEND IT FLYING UP QUICKLY OVER THE HIGH WALL

REAR

FRONT

WHETHER YOU LOOK AT THE FRONT OR BACK OF THE GOLF BALL TRULY MAKES A DIFFERENCE ON FAIRWAY SAND SHOTS.

130 YARDS

ON A PAR-5, WHEN HITTING A FAIRWAY WOOD SECOND SHOT OVER A LOW-LIPPED BUNKER, FOCUS INTENTLY ON THE FRONT OF THE BALL. THIS WAY OF LOOKING ENCOURAGES THE SWEEPING ACTION YOU NEED TO SEND THE BALL FAR DOWN THE FAIRWAY.

The downhill puzzle

MANY AMATEUR GOLFERS CATCH THE BALL THIN OFF DOWNHILL LIES BECAUSE THEY PLAY THE BALL TOO FAR FORWARD IN THE STANCE. WHEN YOU PLAY THE BALL "UP" OFF A STEEP SLOPE, IT'S TOUGH TO MAKE SOLID CONTACT.

SO, PLAY THE BALL A HAIR BEHIND THE MIDWAY POINT IN YOUR STANCE, ALSO SET YOUR BODY PARALLEL TO THE SLOPE AND PUT MORE WEIGHT ON YOUR LEFT FOOT. NOW, YOU'LL STRIKE THE BALL BEFORE THE TURF.

TO HIT AN IRON SHOT THAT "BITES", OR STOPS QUICKLY ON THE GREEN YOU MUST MAKE VERY SHARP CONTACT WITH THE BALL AT IMPACT. TO HIT WITH A DESCENDING BLOW;

1. PUT MORE OF YOUR WEIGHT ON YOUR LEFT FOOT AT ADDRESS
2. PLAY THE BALL BACK IN YOUR STANCE WITH YOUR HANDS AHEAD OF IT;

3. SWING THE CLUB BACK ON AN EXAGGERATED UPRIGHT PLANE;

4. LEAD THE BLADE INTO THE BALL WITH YOUR HANDS.

The stroke-saving pitch

A PITCH SHOT OVER A WATER HAZARD FRIGHTENS THE AVERAGE CLUB PLAYER, HOWEVER DON'T YOU BE AFRAID OF IT.

THIS IS A VERY SIMPLE SHOT PROVIDED YOU GRIP THE HANDLE **LIGHTLY**.

A LIGHT HOLD RELAXES YOUR MUSCLES AND PROMOTES THE LOOSE STEEP UP AND DOWN SWING YOU NEED FOR PERFECTLY EXECUTING THIS SHOT.

PROBLEMS

Judging distances

THE MOST DIFFICULT ADJUSTMENT A GOLFER MUST MAKE WHEN PLAYING A LINKS COURSE IS JUDGING DISTANCES. SINCE THESE TYPES OF COURSES ARE OPEN, FLAT AND FEATURE NO TREES IN THE BACKGROUND OF GREENS, DEPTH PERCEPTION IS SO SEVERELY AFFECTED THAT JUDGING A PITCH SHOT BECOMES ESPECIALLY DIFFICULT. MOST OF THE TIME A GOLFER PLAYING A PITCH HITS THE BALL WELL SHORT OF THE HOLE.

TO HELP YOU PUT A LITTLE MORE POWER INTO YOUR PITCHES AND HIT THE BALL ALL THE WAY TO THE HOLE, AIM FOR THE TOP OF THE FLAG.

Chipping from a downhill lie

IF CHIPPING TO THE HOLE WHEN THE BALL IS AT THE BASE OF A STEEP DOWNHILL SLOPE, VISUALISE A VERY POSITIVE RESULT.

NEXT, SELECT A PITCHING WEDGE. THEN WITH THE BALL BACK, SET UP OPEN. PICK THE CLUB UP QUICKLY.....

ALLOWING YOUR WRISTS TO COCK EARLY IN THE TAKEAWAY.

ON THE DOWNSWING, FEEL AS IF YOU ARE DROPPING THE CLUB INTO THE GRASS DIRECTLY BEHIND THE BALL.